I love her interactive teaching and constructive suggestions that allow the actor to make their own choices. You can absolutely see Judy's years of experience and value from the moment the class begins. Just effortless!

--Krissy Eaton
Agent, Pantheon Talent Agency

I took Judy's class a few months ago. Thanks to Judy's class, I kept it real for an audition and callback a few weeks ago. Booked my 1st National spot, for a huge campaign for Abbvie. Shot it last week. Thanks, Judy!

--Randy Fratkin

I've taken Judy Kain's classes twice. Immediately after ending the first round of classes I was getting callbacks instantly. The second time I was in class within the first week I had a booking! I absolutely attribute my success so far to what I learned with Judy. This class is gold!

--Zach Book

Clearly, Judy is an expert.... No matter how good you are, Judy Kain will help you to be better.

--Genia M.

Not only does Judy provide a solid foundation for actors, she is a supportive, enthusiastic teacher who knows EXACTLY what the commercial world is looking for!!

--Stephanie Burns,
AGENT Avalon Artists Agency

As a talent manager for youth, I am very selective where I send my clients for training. After all, managers don't benefit until our clients book roles, and it's crucial that the talent we represent properly develop and grow in the craft of acting. I have known Judy Kain for many years, and I have to say that she is always on the top of my referral list. The results of her acting program speak for itself and I see the bookings. Judy herself is a class act. Her dignity and reputation in this industry has been nothing short of rock solid!

--Linda Henrie
Go Talent Management

Judy is amazing! Here's some of what you'll learn: -How to prepare for every type of commercial audition -What CD's love (and what they hate) -How to know your type and use it to your advantage -Improvisation Skills for fresh, flexible auditions -Simple, easy "tricks" to nail it in one take. They even helped set up the unrepresented among us with agents- To me, that's above and beyond. Highly Recommended!!!

--Justin B.

Judy Kain, aka the best damn commercial acting coach in the world!

--Don E.

Judy is an insanely gifted teacher, mentor and coach. It's always amazing to see how guidance, when given uncondi- tionally from the heart, can empower someone to be their best in every possible way. Thank you for always seeing our strengths and giving us the courage to use them.

--Natasha A.

Judy gave me the confidence and the technique to book commercial work. She has a system that works for new comers and for pros. 'Find the funny'. Thanks Judy!

--Eric S.
(Booked 10 Commercials the year following this class)

Thank you for giving me pointers on the little things that made a huge difference in my audition techniques. You cut to the chase and it helped me to see things more clearly."

--Germany K.

Callback after callback, avail after avail and still I was not booking. Judy Kain's help tipped the scales in my favor. Bud Light, Budweiser, Apple, Volkswagen, Hershey's, Bud Select 55 and Living Social all in just the last year.

--Christian Z.

"Ever since I took Judy Kain's commercial Intensive, I've booked Apple, McDonalds, Home Depot, Chevy and was on avail for IMS. I have Judy to thank for fueling the fire in my commercial career!"

--Patricia F.

I BOOKED IT

THE COMMERCIAL ACTOR'S HANDBOOK

JUDY KAIN

Keep It Real Acting
North Hollywood, California

© 2015 Judy Kain

Keep It Real Acting
4444 Lankersham Boulevard
Suite 203
North Hollywood, CA 91602
keepitreal@keepitrealacting.com

All rights reserved. No part of this book may be reproduced, stored in a retrieval system, or transmitted in any form or by any means—electronic or mechanical, photocopy, recording, or any other—except for brief quotations in printed reviews, without the prior permission of the publisher. Although the author and publisher have made every effort to ensure the accuracy and completeness of information contained in this book, we assume no responsibility for errors, inaccuracies, omissions, or any inconsistency herein.

ISBN: 978-1-938620-13-3

Published by Keep It Real Acting, North Hollywood, CA
an imprint of Westcom Press, Washington, DC

Cataloging-in-Publication data for this book is available
from the Library of Congress

Printed in United States of America

Cover Design: Katy Bodenhamer - Bodenhamer Design
                 bodenhamerdesign@gmail.com

Interior Layout: Westcom Associates
                 westcomassociates@mac.com

Dedication

This book is dedicated to:

Carolyne Barry, who passed away in 2015. She was my mentor, my first commercial teacher, and my colleague, and she gave me hope and belief in myself.

My students, past, present and future. As you continue to book commercials, you prove my techniques work and are teachable.

Acknowledgements

This book would not have become a reality without the generous help of a large, diverse group of people. I thank you all:

First and foremost, my commercial agents at Brady, Brannon & Rich, who continue to believe in me after all these years. Francene Selkirk, for her help & support with her vast skills she employed while teaching with me for over ten years. And Danielle Eskinazi for being a ridiculously talented Casting Director and source of support.

All the directors, casting directors, and producers who have hired me over the years. I appreciate that you always think of me!

My staff and teachers at Keep it Real Acting Studios for your never-ending dedication to the studio: Jessica Lynn Verdi, Katy Bodenhamer, Beau Brians, Stacy Edwards, Paul Hungerford, Doug Traer, Nancy Linari, Donna Rusch, Suzanne Schmidt, Randall Sims, Tremayne Woodard, April Baker, Nicole DaCosta and Tom Burke.

Bredgette Brookman, who set aside a few hours a week to show up and hold me accountable as I wrote this book.

Tom Stern and Michael Vezo for their support in getting this book done!

Ross Lacy, Kevin Emmons, Hugh Leon and Anton Maile for their amazing contribution to the book.

And my first commercial teacher and mentor Carolyne Barry who passed away in 2015. She gave me hope, belief in myself and the skills I need to **book it!**

Contents

Introduction

Commercials! Some people fast-forward through them, some turn their nose up at them, but thousands of actors compete to be in them.

Commercials are everywhere . . . in the movie theaters before the main feature . . . on your iPad while you're playing a game . . . incessantly popping up on the internet before you can watch *anything* online . . . even on monitors at the grocery store checkout line. Commercials are not just on TV anymore.

Personally, I love commercials, and not just at Super Bowl time. They make me laugh with their clever themes, make me tear up with their sincerity, and inform me of products I have to have. But, most important, I love to be in them!

Nothing feels better than when my agent calls and lets me know **I booked it**!

Now don't get me wrong—I didn't always start out with this attitude. As a classically trained young actor, I performed Molière and Shaw and worked out with the Polish lab *Theatre,* performing Grotowski in the industrial lofts in Berkley.

In addition to performing various types of experimental theatre, I studied the classics, including Federico Garcia Lorca, Tennessee Williams, and Henrik Ibsen. I graduated at the top of my class from University of Wisconsin/Milwaukee with a Bachelor of Fine Arts degree, and my goal was to do repertory theater around the U.S.

The universe had other plans for me, apparently. I landed in Los Angeles by chance, driving down from Berkeley one weekend to help a friend rehearse for an audition. The next thing I knew, I was living in a furnished apartment on Franklin and La Brea, and as a bonus, the complex had a pool.

While I got my start in a dozen or so equity waiver shows at LACC, MATRIX, and the GNU Theatre, at the same time I signed up with an acting school called The Faculty, headed up by New York renegades from Herbert Berghoff Studios. The amazing Ken McMillan taught an exceptionally great scene study class that I took for years.

On a fluke, I added an acting technique class with Dena Dietrich, the actress who became known as Mother Nature in the Chiffon Margarine commercials back in the late 70s. Dena was the one who inspired me to get a start in commercials. She was a real actress who landed some amazing commercials. With her encouragement, I set about on my quest to conquer the commercial world.

After being told by several reputable agents that I was not a commercial type, I was fortunate to land an agent to represent me—Judy Rich at Commercials Unlimited.

Excited and full of exuberance, I went out on auditions. The first six months, I didn't get a booking. I am an Aries and like to master whatever it is I do, so I signed up for a class with the late, great Carolyne Barry to learn the craft of commercial acting. Carolyne taught me what I needed to know about auditioning, and she gave me confidence to bring to every audition.

Just as I finished the eight-week commercial class, I got the dreaded letter from my agent: Commercials Unlimited was dropping me. I was devastated. I knew that Carolyne's class gave me an understanding of the art form of commercials, and now I needed to test out my new-found skill set. In desperation, I did something that I still look back on as a ballsy move: I asked Judy Rich to give me another chance. To my surprise and relief, she responded with a cool, "Okay; I'll give you three more months, and we'll see what happens."

Within a week of that call I booked a national spot, and I have been loyal to Judy Rich ever since. She is still my agent today.

My first booking was for Corning Eyeglasses, and the spot took place in a nudist colony, Hollywood's version of the Garden of Eden. My character was Eve, and of course my scene partner was Adam. It was a very funny spot about eyeglasses with lenses that changed from clear to dark; the slogan was "You never have to take them off!"

I was so thrilled to be in this big national spot that I didn't really read the fine print. I had to be practically naked to shoot this spot. As a matter of fact, the only items that kept me from really looking like the original Eve were two pasties and a little G-string. Fortunately, I was in my early 20s and had little to hide at that point. Most of the time my character was shielded by a newspaper, and Adam was covered by a large fig leaf.

My favorite moment in the shoot was the final shot; Adam and I were walking away from the camera on the nature trail, with a live moose conveniently positioned to hide our backsides from the camera. On one take, we were strolling down the path when the moose decided to just walk off, exposing our buttocks for everyone to see.

Although that take, thankfully, was not in the final edit of the commercial, the popular TV show *Bloopers and Bleepers* somehow picked it up. The moonshot segment with the moose walking out of the frame aired for two years on national television.

To date, I have played everything from a super-hero hotline operator for Starz Network to a dancing lobster for a local seafood restaurant. I have been in several Super Bowl commercials and many Cleo-winning spots. On the other hand, I must admit that I've been left on the cutting room floor a few times as well.

I've played waitresses, teachers, librarians, mean bosses, nosy neighbors, and frazzled moms. I've flown all over the country to shoots, worked with some amazing directors and fellow actors, and met and worked with amazing celebrities. I am proud of the work I have done in commercials, and I look forward to sharing what I've learned with you.

The one thing I know for a fact is that there is technique and skill to auditioning for commercials.

My book and my experience can help you master the audition process and get you on the set of many, many commercials.

Prepare for a great ride and let's get down to the basics of commercial auditioning.

Chapter 1

Commercial Acting— Training is Essential

Use what you know. Don't worry about what you don't know.
—Michael Shurtleff, playwright, casting director, and author

Maybe your friends tell you, "You're so attractive, you should be in commercials!" Or perhaps you've been approached at the mall by a talent agent who says your child is a natural and it'll be easy to get her into commercials.

Acting in commercials has the lure of seeming to be a simple profession. Everyone believes it's easy to get into, easy to achieve quick success, and of course you will make piles of money!

But as commercial director Kevin Emmons says about a British actor: "I was working with this actor on a shoot. He was classically trained and brilliant, and he is now suddenly in front of a teleprompter with all these lines, and he has to do this specific action while walking and talking . . . and by the third take he was overwhelmed. He said he acted his whole life and this [commercial stuff] is hard!"

Good actors make commercial acting look easy. However, saying words that are product-driven with little-to-no time to practice or rehearse, getting virtually no background explanation whatsoever, making it look like you're having an everyday conversation with a friend in front of complete strangers while the camera is rolling—it is all a lot more challenging than it looks.

A student in his late 50s took my 6-week A-Z commercial class. He was a successful ear/nose/throat surgeon, and typically impatient. After the final class he asked, "How long does it take to get a job?"

"Well, how long did it take you before you began practicing surgery?" I asked with a smile.

He said, "Four years of college, two years of grad school and four years in a residency."

"Okay, and so what makes you think you can master commercial acting in six weeks?" I said with a little glint in my eye and steel in my tone. He was speechless.

Casting director Ross Lacy told me once, "I always laugh when someone says, 'Omigosh, I would like to be in commercials,' and I say, 'Sure you would! So would everybody. That's why these people are training and go to improv classes all night long because they make it look easy—and it's not! And the people who think it is are mistaken!'

Ross continues, "The one thing I know is that training

is imperative if you want a lasting career in commercials. Of course there are stories of the person who walked in, booked the job, and made a pile of money off one spot. This is definitely the exception. The same odds apply to winning the lottery."

Just like my acting student/surgeon, most people wouldn't dream of trying to start a new career in any field *other* than acting without getting the proper training, doing whatever it takes to make themselves competitive.

Study the Craft of Acting

Honestly, the best teacher of commercial acting is the commercial itself. *Watch* commercials, *study* them, and *find yourself* in them. Put the remote down and watch the stories being told in the amazing 30-second short films called commercials. There is much to be learned via this exercise, from tone and style, to how to dress for commercials, to how to wear your hair, to the nuances of an understated performance.

Find a class that can give you solid, specific, on-camera training for the art form of auditioning for commercials. For a small investment, you can find out in six to eight weeks if this is something for which you have a passion and ability. You will be able to get some insights as to what will be in store for you.

A commercial acting class should always be done on camera, or, in my opinion, it's a waste of your time. Since every audition is done on camera, it's completely unrealistic to study without using one. The most important things you'll take away from your commercial class will be how to:

- Approach commercial copy
- Use a cue card
- Make the camera your friend

You'll also need to take some acting technique classes to give yourself a strong technical foundation. Acting is acting, whether it's drama, comedy, commercials, films, on the stage, or for television. Your job is to be authentic, connected and present within the confines of the scene, whether it's Shakespeare or a 15-second commercial.

As a well-rounded acting student, you'll become a quality actor who happens to do commercials.

Evaluate available acting classes using these key criteria:

Take a class from a working pro

Your best choice is a class taught by someone who is currently doing what they are teaching. You get firsthand experience from a professional who is active and successful in the subject being taught. A long as they still love what they do, you will be in good hands. Check out the instructor on the IMDb (Internet Movie Database), and run their name by several different sources, ideally working commercial casting directors or agents who are active in commercials.

Take a class in a studio with professional camera and monitor

You must be able to see what you and others are doing through the eye of the camera. Since auditions for commercials are always done on camera, it is crazy to take classes without actually working in front of one. You'll learn what works and doesn't simply by watching the other students. Most classes should offer a recording for you to review and see your growth.

Make sure the copy being used fits current trends

Commercial trends change quickly, and current copy is critical for you to practice for the auditions you will have. These days, most commercials don't even mention the product in the spot. Only the voiced-over tag tells us what the product is.

Class should be minimum of 6-8 weeks long

You cannot learn everything you need to build a sustained career in a one-day seminar. You may become inspired or motivated in a day, but you won't be trained. There are at least five different types of commercial auditions, and different techniques specifically apply to each of the five types. Building skill upon skill is critical for a confident commercial actor.

These new skills take time to develop and they are critical to know. Some techniques you will only do in an audition and nowhere else. For example, in an audition you have to motivate out towards the camera. You would never do it on the actual set, or even during a theatrical interview, but at a commercial interview, it's vital that you motivate towards the camera so you can be seen.

Meet an industry guest

An industry person should be scheduled to come in at the end of class so you can make connections. You have heard the adage, *It is who you know in this town.* Unfortunately, it's true! You want to build relationships based on your talent. So take a class, hone your skills, and then meet those who have the power to bring you in. *Don't* meet them before you study—you want your first impression to be a good as well as a lasting one.

This is just the beginning of your commercial training. Start with the basics to get you going, then you will find that you need to take some improvisation to loosen you up. Improv training will add a layer of spontaneity and quick subtle responses to your acting when you do auditions.

You may find that you are not getting enough bookings and may need to take an advanced class to help you turn callbacks into bookings. Or perhaps you'll need to spend a year or two in a theatrical technique class to learn how to access your emotions.

At some point, we actors often feel we no longer need to continue training. Always remember that is *not* the case. Classes refresh a tired performance, classes give us new perspective, and most definitely, classes rid of us of our bad habits.

Equate acting classes to gym workouts—you know what happens when we stop going there! Our muscles get weak, flab starts to appear and we lose our momentum. The same thing happens when we take a break from class. Our acting techniques become soft and out of shape.

You never know when you'll have a chance at an audition. You want to be on the top of your game at that moment—you don't want to be in a slump!

Do your research. Find a class that suits your needs.

Chapter 2

What's the Secret to Booking a Job?

I'm a skilled professional actor. Whether or not
I've any talent is beside the point.
—Sir Michael Caine, actor and author

After a long day at work, you kick back, turn on the TV, and start flipping through the channels. If you have a good eye, you will start to recognize the same actors in a variety of commercials.

Why do you think those actors have more success in booking commercial jobs?

- Their look
- They are the type the director is looking for
- They said all the words on the script
- They said it all in under 30 seconds

Surprise! It's actually none of the above. Actors have the misconception that directors and agency people know what they are looking for in each role. The directors and agency people may have a concept or an idea, but they really don't know what they want until they see it walk into the room and be brought to life.

The actor who brings the spot to life with his own unique perspective generally gets the part. In other words, **personality** is the key. Personality coupled with technique and confidence is intoxicating in an audition.

The easy part is that you already have a distinctive, individual personality. The challenge is that it's your job to bring it to every audition you go to!

Who you are as a person is your biggest asset. Personality—the compilation of your interpretations, your uniqueness, your charm—*that* is what books jobs. No, it's not your ability to memorize lines. Your look is part of your personality. You will get callbacks because you committed to your choices and engaged them with your interpretation. You want to incorporate your special qualities, your competitive edge, and your castable self into every spot when you audition.

When they call your name and you go into the audition room, you will go stand on the *mark* (a spot or tape line on the floor), and you will be asked to *slate* your name. This is how you introduce yourself to the director, client and agency who will review the tape. The slate is the first time the decision-makers see you, so it is an opportunity to show your personality. You look right into the camera lens, and you need to maintain the connection with confidence and energy.

In my classes, I ask actors to think of someone they always wanted to meet, then imagine that person is just a couple of feet in front of them inside the camera lens. I often use Brad Pitt as my person in the lens; he always makes me smile and brings out a side of me that I think is charming. I'm glowing because I truly want to be there with Mr. Pitt, but the director thinks I'm glowing admiringly at him.

Who would give you the most thrills and chills to meet? When the session director asks for your name, visualize that amazing person asking for your name and respond to that person instead.

If you wear glasses, they may ask you to take them off for a moment so you can be seen without them, then you can put your glasses back on so you can see.

Here are some more tips for a great slate:

- Slating is introducing yourself to someone you really want to meet.
- You're thrilled to meet this person!
- Choose a few people you will be blown away to meet and put them in the audition camera.
- Get loose before you slate; let go of all stress. Have no tension in your face.
- Keep your hands free.
- Focus on the person you are meeting in the camera.
- Say "Hello. Hi! How're you doing?"
- And then you say your name.

Often you will be asked for left and right profiles, views of you from each side. Don't drop your energy when you look to each side, away from the camera. You want to keep that fantastic person in mind as you turn so you continue to see them when you look away. *This is NOT a mug shot!*

Don't do profiles unless you're asked, and when you are, don't belabor it. Turn for just a brief showing of each side. When passing through the middle, make sure you connect with camera again.

They may also ask to see your hands. Just hold them up in front of your face and show both sides. This is not to see if you had a manicure, so there's no need to mention your unkempt cuticles. They just need to verify that you have five fingers and no glaring scars or tattoos. If you do, that is not a problem either. They will just have to cover them before the shoot.

First calls are much more relaxed than the callbacks, which we will talk about later. Generally, it's just you and the session director, who is hired by the commercial casting director to put the actors on tape.

Just a little personal advice: Ask the session directors for their names and write them down. The next time you see them, remember their name and ask how they're doing. Everyone believes you need to know and develop a relationship with the casting director, but session directors are the gatekeepers to casting directors. Be respectful and treat them well, and you may be pleasantly surprised at the results.

Session directors are a very important part of the audition; they can make or break an audition for you. Session directors are there to get a good performance from you for the best take, the one that goes to the director. They want you to be great! They can give you the tips and direction you need to score a callback. They are not, however, going to spend a ton of time to help you get there.

In the first call, all questions and rehearsals are only seen and heard by the session director. Don't be afraid to ask questions: What's the style and tone of the piece? Is there room for comedy? These questions will allow you to get more info and process it in your body before you begin. You do need to be prepared and have choices; we'll talk about this next.

Chapter 3

The Audition

Forget the career, do the work. If you feel what you are doing is on line and you're going someplace and you have a vision and you stay with it, eventually things will happen.

—Al Pacino, actor, director and producer

Inevitably, you will be called to a commercial audition at the most inconvenient time, to the farthest location from where you live. Of course, because over 2,500 actors are submitted for each role by their agents, and *you* were lucky enough to get picked, you happily change your hair appointment, reschedule lunch with your boyfriend, and even cancel the fun getaway to the beach.

I always look at auditions both as an opportunity to act and as a potential job. You ought to take any audition seriously and give it 150%. In other words, prepare in any and all ways you can for the audition.

Do your due diligence

Look up recent commercials for the client. If the audition is for a Best Buy commercial, for example, look up their commercials on YouTube and see if there is a common theme.

Find out if copy is available before the audition, and if so, start to prepare. It may be sent to you or be available online.

Choose the right outfit to wear. Students often ask if you can go too far for a commercial audition. I say loudly, **NO!** You can go all the way with that waitress outfit. Always keep in mind, though, that you want to look like a real person, not a parody. That is the key—you must look like you really *are* a waitress, or a nurse, or a housewife in the Midwest.

If you were going to a job interview, you would definitely make an effort and wear heels or a jacket and tie. So don't cut corners and just wear whatever you have on that day unless it is literally a last-minute audition and you can't go home first.

The five types of commercial auditions

There are five very distinct and different types of auditions. We will cover each type in depth in separate chapters, and you'll learn the specific techniques you need to know for each one in order to book the job.

- *MOS:* You don't speak words, but you're given a specific scenario.

- *Improv:* You're given a specific scenario, but they will have you add your own dialogue
- *Spokesperson:* You'll be alone, doing all the talking
- *Scenes:* You'll interact with two or more actors.
- *Personality slate or interview:* You will be asked a random question.

For four types of audition —all except the personality question —you will also want to employ the following basic tools to prepare.

Prepare for your role

You must read all the material for the commercial and understand your role. Most actors overlook this part, and it costs them.

If the material isn't available online or sent to you in advance, you must allow extra time on audition day. Don't sign in when you arrive! Show up early, grab the copy before signing in, go back outside or to the bathroom, and start working on it. If the casting assistant spots you, simply ask if you can run to the bathroom. I *never* ask for a minute with the copy, I just grab it and hide out of sight. If you're not signed in, you're not there in the casting office's eyes. You can take the much-needed time to prepare—as long as you sign in before your assigned call time.

Here are the steps you take, whether or not you have time to do it in advance:

Read and understand

Start by reading the entire sides, storyboard or description. Make sure you read *all lines* and *all notes* so you can determine the tone of the piece. Is it a slice of life? Is it far-fetched, but you need to play it real? Is it testimonial or interview style? It really helps if you've studied commercials and can recognize the different styles and tones.

See how your character services the scene, where you fit in from the directorial perspective.

This is also the time to do a quick Google search if you are unfamiliar with anything that is in the copy.

Once you understand the role, it's time for the three P's: paraphrase, personalize, practice!

Paraphrase

Put the scene in your own words. Make it your own and know exactly what it is you're doing in this place. This is an excellent way to memorize the lines as they will make much more sense to you if you make this a regular practice. It's miraculous, but if you really know what you're saying, you'll be able to remember it.

Use the worksheet in this chapter; make specific choices about where you are, what you want, and why you are saying what you are saying. Know who you're talking to.

Is there room for comedy? I believe a little comedy can be found in most spots. It's a great asset to find it and incorporate some irony or a comedic twist into a moment of the commercial. Studying improvisation can truly help you with this in your auditions.

As you paraphrase, though, refrain from sounding "selly." The tone in today's commercials is very filmic, and often the product is not even mentioned by anyone in the scene, just voiced over at the end. *Never, never, EVER sell*. That is not your job; it's the advertiser's job. Your job is to play the scene and work to get what you want from the person you're talking to.

Personalize

This is where you can add your own experience as it fits within the confines of the scene. You always want to work within the framework of the scene you are given; just put your own spin on it or infuse a little hint of your personality into the scene.

This is very important: It is *your* audition, and your job is to lift the copy from the page and make it come alive. You do this by making everything you are talking about *personal*. Pick someone from your life to talk to. I have a list of five to seven people to whom I talk on a regular basis during my scenes; I use them and actually cast them in the scene.

You should choose real people who are a part of your life, not made-up people. If you're talking about a child of yours and you don't have children, the scene is not going to be real for you. So cast a child you know, maybe your niece, or the neighbors' child that you're close to, one who elicits a warm feeling. Talk to the real person and see how the scene becomes more real for you. Say their name out loud before you say the first line of dialogue, and you can connect more easily.

You must know how you feel about everything you talk about in the commercial. We are opinionated people, so how is it possible to have no point of view whatsoever when we read copy? No, it's not possible! Have a strong point of view just like you do in life. Just avoid anger and lean more towards the positive spectrum.

Prepare a few approaches to the material; be an actor with many ways to go. Have several choices of people you can talk to and reasons why you are saying these words; this will make you a very directable actor. Don't get stuck doing it one way, unable to take notes and change.

Make the copy your own by lifting it off the page with your unique personality. Because you have lived a full life, you are able to bring your own perspective to every spot. Remember they want to see *you* and how *you* would say these words based on your life experience. Don't default to a cookie cutter approach. Use your life and experience on each audition.

Prepare *buttons* and *tags*, one for each scenario. They can be verbal or physical; however I prefer to do a verbal one when appropriate. This allows me to give a bit of my personality and point of view more readily. Think of the button as the next thing you would say, after the last scripted line.

Practice

Get the words out of your mouth before you go into your audition. You do not want the words coming out of your mouth for the first time on your first take... **disaster**!

Say the words at full volume. Words sound different vocalized than they do up in your head.

Launch into the first line of dialogue; know what happened to motivate the first line. Make sure you see something, hear something being said, or think something that motivates you to launch into the first line of dialogue. Feel free to add a word or two that allows you to really launch yourself into the first line.

Memorize the first and last line of copy so you can direct those lines into camera, or directly to the person you have chosen to talk to. Then make the cue card part of your fourth wall. In this way you give yourself permission to look at the cue card as part of your scene rather than break character and drop out of the scene to pick up your line. If your scene is in a coffee shop, make the cue card the menu or the blackboard. Or the case of baked goods . . . or a cute barista you are checking out.

Once you are called into the room, **ask for a rehearsal**. At the least, look at the cue card and do a quick take out loud while the session director is finding your name on the call sheet. It is a free take; you might even get some notes from the session director! Make the most of it. You'll be lucky to get two official takes once you're called.

When your moment comes, though, it is time to let the work go. Relax, start the audition with confidence. Have fun, and trust all the work you did, it's time to enjoy the art of acting. Auditions are an opportunity to act. Seize the opportunity and use your gifts. Don't think about getting the job, or question whether you did it right. Just play the scene, breathe, and breathe life into the script and lift it off the page. Focus on who you are.

Leave on an upbeat note, get in your car, and let it go. Your work is done. The rest is out of your control.

Review your audition prep

- Research the client's commercials.
- Choose the right outfit to wear.
- Read the material. Understand what you are saying and/or doing in the scene.
- Find the tone of the piece.
- Paraphrase the copy.
- See if there is room for comedy.
- Use the worksheet, page 29.
- Try a few approaches to the material.
- Make it your own by lifting it off the page in your style.
- Launch into the first line of dialogue,
- Have buttons and tags—one for each scenario. They can be verbal or physical.
- Memorize the first and last line of copy.
- Get up and rehearse.
- Relax and enjoy the acting.

KEEP IT REAL Commercial Worksheet

Read the copy. Paraphrase the script in your own words. Paraphrase again with 90% script, 10% your own words. Fill out sheet two different ways for every spot. Rehearse out loud several times. Release and be willing to have fun!

Version 1

Who are you talking to?_____

Where are you? _____

What do you want? _____

What are you doing? _____

How do you feel about him/her/it? _____

What launches you into copy? _____

Buttons _____

Version 2

Who are you talking to? _____

Where are you? _____

What do you want? _____

What are you doing? _____

How do you feel about him/her/it? _____

What launches you into copy? _____

Buttons _____

Q&A With Commercial Casting Director Ross Lacy

Ross Lacy is one of the most successful Commercial casting directors in Los Angeles. Here is what he has to say about Commercial casting.

A casting director is hired by a production company or commercial director to find appropriate talent (actors and actresses) to audition for commercial projects and put them on tape for the director and clients to see. Every city with commercial products has a multitude of casting directors serving as the gatekeepers between the production company and an actor's agent.

Once casting directors are hired for a commercial, they send a breakdown of all the spot's roles out to agencies; the agents select clients who are right for the roles. The casting director then narrows down 2,500-3,000 submissions, choosing 50-100 actors to come in and read for each role.

Relationships with casting directors are key for an actor to continue to work. Developing those relationships can take time.

Judy: What do you love about casting commercials?
Ross: I *love* casting commercials because they are fast-paced compared to a theatrical thing; I like the turn-around. A long job in a commercial is two weeks, and most jobs are four days.

We got a call today to prep a job; we'll cast on Tuesday and Wednesday and do callbacks on Friday. That's typical.

Judy: What skills make a casting director?

Ross: In commercial casting, it is multitasking, especially now with the way we are casting online. It's sooooo fast . . . and it's a 24-hour job! It is constant emails through the night. You finally turn it off, and they're there waiting for you in the morning.

It really is constant, especially because you do production with companies overseas or with Australia and New Zealand. It keeps going and going, and the clients are so used to getting things right away now, that the pace is ramped up.

When I started 20 years ago, we used ¾-inch tapes, then DVDs, and now it's posting. Clients didn't use to expect that kind of speed and now they do.

So multitasking and keeping everybody happy are important. But ultimately the skill we need is knowing the talent. You need to know the talent, especially with the way things go so fast now, when they say, "Hey, we need x, y, and z *right now!*" To know the talent and the base, call the right agent and get those people in is super important.

Judy: Can you give us an overview of the casting process?

Ross: It starts when I'm put on hold for a job; usually it comes from a production company because it's a director I work with. I don't bid on the job.

Once the job awards, they send me specs and boards, and I get on the phone.

For me it is about contacts. I am starting a job with a new director I have been dying to work for, but it is because he has seen my work and he'd like to see those people and those faces.

Our work is a little bit of everything, not just one type of thing. We do beauty and comedy and dry spots and vignette spots. Each depends on looking at the director's body of work—each director is different.

We talk about the specs and agree on what we're looking for. I learned this from a director when I first started. He wanted a pretty girl for this commercial, and I kept bring him in what *I* thought was pretty—but he really thought a pretty girl was a super tomboy type. It took me a couple days to figure that out, as he was getting madder about what I was bringing in.

I always equate casting as like a game of Telephone, because the ad agency has sold it, the client and the client have approved it, then they talk about it to the director, and then the director talked to me. The dissemination of information changes every step of the way.

So part of it is knowing what this director thinks is pretty or what the spot needs. We get on the phone, we talk about the specs and try to figure it out so we get it right, and then I put a breakdown out online. I'll say, "I want a banal cubicle worker, 30-35, all ethnicities," and send it out to the agents.

The agents submit their clients online, we go through the pictures and pick the actors we like or know or think would be right for the job.

It is a fine balance. Actors come in and say "My agent is not submitting me," and they are angry at their agents, and no, your agent *is* submitting you. You just may not be right for what we are doing.

All actors think they are right for everything.

When we get 3,000 pictures for that role and we can only see 100 people, it is our job to cull it down. What you do is you have to balance it. Of the 100 that we will see, I bring in 30 whom I know and love, who may be a little exposed but I know they can do the job, and I know they are going to be great. I'll also bring in 30 people I want to try out —new faces —because you want to continually show the director new faces, and also because it helps all of us.

We hold the auditions and have the actors come in, we videotape them and send the link to the director. They watch the link and they give us their selects. Out of the original 100, the agency and director each pick ten. We have a callback for those 20 people, and out of those 20, one person books it!

The number has gone from 3,000 to 100 to 20, down to one.

Judy: What about avails (backups)?
Ross: It depends on the job. We just did a huge Samsung

job with 52 principles, so there was a backup pool of people so if we lose someone we can slot in.

In general, you will have a first choice, a backup and an alternate.

Judy: How much is personality and how much is talent?
Ross: It depends on the job. Some of the vignette stuff we do—when we do interviews and we just talk to people—it could be personality. If it is a dialogue piece, it comes down to training and improv skills.

I always laugh when someone says, "Oh, my gosh, I would like to be in commercials!" And I say, "Sure you would. So would everybody, that why these people are training and go to improv classes all night long and they make it look easy—and it's not!" The people who think it's easy are mistaken.

Judy: Tell me the ways actors blow a job.
Ross: Actors can shoot themselves in the foot for sure. They come in and talk too much. The kiss of death is to talk about how great the real product is, like, "Oh, man, I really do drink Budweiser!"

Some of it comes down to the fact that the agency and the director are all going to be hanging out with you for 12 hours a day when you're shooting. If there are two choices and one of them is friendly and nice and the one of them is annoying (and they both can do the job), then definitely the friendly, nice one is going to get the job, because it comes down to who do I want to spend my day with.

So personality does come into play. You don't want to overstep your bounds—you don't know us that well, we are not your friends at that moment, you're there in the audition room to do a good job, but that doesn't mean you can't be personal and get a laugh out of us, but read the room and act accordingly. Keep it professional.

Judy: When you're looking at submissions, what stands out?
Ross: *An actor should not pick their own picture!* Your image of yourself is very different from the truth. The kiss of death is when an actor comes into my office. If I see your picture and I say, "Oh my god, this person is perfect," I am going to give you one of these valuable 100 slots. Then you come in, and I am like, "Who is this person? This is not *that* person! That is not this person at all!" That stands out in my mind more than anything, because I have wasted time.

The headshot should be an accurate representation of not only what you look like, but of who you are!

The days of the big smiley commercial shots are gone. It shouldn't feel like you're trying too hard. Remember, too, that pictures can't be *too* perfect —makeup too perfect, hair too perfect. It comes off overdone, as though you're trying too hard. I much prefer natural. Your hair should be like it would be if you come in here.

The pictures are not for the agents. They are for **us**. For casting.

Judy: How can an actor improve his odds of getting chosen for a callback?

Ross: Listen, it is really simple, to be dead honest. I like an actor to come in to the audition room prepared by reading the boards and everything we give to you out in the lobby. I pride my office on being one that supplies information to actors. It doesn't come off as a good audition if you don't have the information. The way I continue to get more jobs is by doing a good job and sending that link out at night.

We need you guys as much as you need us, so I want to give you the best opportunity when you're in there. Ultimately, that is what we are trying to do.

You actors put yourself on the line so much and it is such a vulnerable place to be. The easiest, safest thing to do to protect yourself is to talk to your friends while you're in the lobby, and come into the room and do a good job, not a great job, not a bad job—it's fine. Then when you don't get the job you say, "You know, I wasn't really prepared. If I really prepared, then I would have gotten the job." But it's scary then; what if you *are* prepared and you don't get the job?

Listen to the people we have in the lobby and the people who run the session; we have access to the director and the client and talk to them, and we know, hopefully, what they are looking for. We are going to give you that information as best we can.

It is not that we want a homogeneous tape; we want you to bring your own vibe or your own unique thing to it. When we talk to you, it's like, "Here are the parameters of what we are looking for, so within those parameters, give us something, but we need you to hit these three beats because we *know* they want that."

I remember doing an improv scene when I was an actor. It was a party scene; everyone was trying to so hard to get noticed, to be seen, thinking here is my opportunity to act, and we were all being loud. And then there was a guy standing against the wall eating chips—he was the person that stood out the most because he wasn't fighting for the attention.

A lot of times in commercials we want you to do less—down, down, down, less, less. Actors come in here, it is their audition for the week, and they're thinking, "Here is my opportunity to act!" We want them to do a deadpan look, a frozen moment, and they say, "Okay, got it," but they are not listening to the direction.

Judy: How does an actor get known by your office?
Ross: Do a good job! There are people we take a liking to, meaning new faces we see, and we'll say, "Hey, let's give them a try." People who come in physically to the office too many times consistently get on our Do Not See list.

If an agent we like says, "Could you see Sarah for this? I really think she is great," we may not put her on our Yes list the first time, but we will probably do it the second time. I really do try to see new people for a certain number of the slots I have, because again, that is important to my director. We rely on the agent for that; we can't be out looking at a thousand people so we do rely on good agents who have someone who they refer and whom they push, and we will try to get them in.

The other thing is being *ready* to audition. People come to LA and say, "I'm here and I need to start auditioning." What stands out is if you do a *bad* job. If you do a medium to good job, that is great —perfect! But if you do a *bad* job, that stands out and then it sticks in our mind. So be ready before you have your agent give it a shot.

Judy: Do you ever look at headshots when people send them to your office?

Ross: We do see them and go through them, and every now and then we'll see someone and think, oh, my *gosh*, that person is perfect for what we doing right now. That does happen. If someone has taken the time to send them, I am going to try to take the time to look at them.

Judy: Do look through all agencies' submissions?

Ross: We *do*. Rarely, maybe once or twice a year, when a job is really fast, we will see just 30% because we don't have time to look through 3000 photos. But in general, it behooves us to look through them.

It is not like there are the top five agencies in town and theirs are the only people we will see. Out of the 484 agencies that are submitting to us, if some are getting five out of the 100 slots, that's a big percentage. We need to see people from smaller places. One of my main directors likes really unusual people so I have to dig deep. On the commercial side, there are 700 agents and managers who are submitting.

About Ross Lacy

 After acting in high school and college in New York, Ross moved to Hollywood to be an actor. He realized he also had skills in casting, and after a year in front of the camera, he got behind the camera first for Mick Dowd Casting, then other casting directors.

He married an actress, and decided one actor in the family is enough. He says, "The bottom line is, I'm better at talking to actors and giving them direction than I am at doing it myself."

Chapter 4

Personality Slate or Interview-Style Audition

Acting is standing up naked and turning around very slowly.
—Rosalind Russel, actor

Interview auditions are usually done in a group, though sometimes you may be interviewed separately. In either case, there's no copy to learn, no scene to play. You're just asked a random question.

I dreaded this type of auditions, and for years I never booked one. I focused obsessively on the questions, and agonized over my answers.

One day, a session director told me that the director and clients often watch these auditions with the volume turned completely off. Immediately, I realized the purpose and potential of the random question. It's all about our **personality**—how we come across on camera.

Using this nugget of information, I changed my whole approach to this audition.

Since it's personality they are looking for, I needed something to talk about that turns me on, that I am passionate about, something I can discuss fluently without worrying or running out of specific details.

Now I always talk about one of three subjects that make my eyes and face light up: hiking, my son, and my dog, Sparky.

To sail through the interview question audition, you must approach it the same way: Choose three things that you are passionate about, subjects you can talk about easily and effortlessly and in detail. The details let your personality shine through. Here are some ideas:

- Your favorite travel destination
- An anecdote about a family member
- A story about your pet
- The joys of your hobby

When asked a question, *any* question, find a quick way to segue or transition into talking about one of your favorite subjects.

Know you do not need to answer the questions. Just transition quickly to your chosen subject.

Keep your answer brief, but detailed and specific. Again do not feel like you have to answer the question correctly. The truth is, they do not care what book you just read—they are just trying to see your personality on camera.

Beware of three taboo subjects—avoid these at all cost

- **Acting.** They want you to be an actor and a skilled one but do not want to hear about it. They secretly think they are discovering you in the local farmers' market and putting you in their commercial campaign.
- **Politics.** Politics are just too controversial and should be avoided at all cost. Even if you're running for senate, leave it alone!
- **Religion.** Anything religious in nature is taboo.

Let's practice. Take a sample question: Seen any good movies lately? Normally you would take a moment to pause, think, "Uh . . . yes, I did see a good movie the other night with Meryl Streep . . . blah blah." You have already lost them, and they lost the opportunity to learn anything about you!

The beauty about this technique is that you never have to think about the answer because you already know it.

Try this instead. "Yes, a hiking documentary. I am an avid hiker and love to get high up any mountain. I guess I'm a sucker for a view. I am training to do Machu Picchu in a few months, and we are going the back route and staying in the mountain lodges in Peru. And the best part is llamas carry our gear. It should be fun and easier than my last hike—Kilimanjaro. That was hard!"

Something like that will get me noticed, because I am engaged from the moment I start talking.

There's no need to repeat the question; it just takes up time.

Practice this technique with some of these commonly-asked questions and see how it works for you!

- What was your best vacation?
- Do you have any hobbies?
- Any plans for the summer?
- What was the last book you read?
- What kind of music do you like?
- Tell us about the worst night out you had.
- Share one of your happiest memories
- What was your most embarrassing moment?
- What happened to you yesterday?
- What kind of foods you love?
- What kind of foods you hat?
- Seen any good movies lately?
- Share your biggest pet peeves.
- Any plans for the holidays?
- Who's the most important person in your life?
- What is your most treasured possession?
- Do you have any bad habits?
- Which is your favorite TV show?

- Have any phobias?
- What is your guilty pleasure?
- Do you work with your hands?
- If you had a super power, what would it be?
- If you could meet anyone dead or alive, who would it be?

Chapter 5

MOS Auditions —No Dialogue

An ounce of behavior is worth a pound of words.
—Sanford Meisner, actor, acting teacher

There's a Hollywood legend about how the term "MOS" came about. Supposedly, a famous director with a heavy German accent announced that he was going to shoot a scene "mit out sound." It's a good story, and a lot funnier than "motor only shot" or some of the other technical terminology the letters may stand for. In any case, MOS spots don't have dialogue; voice-overs or music is added post-production.

Agents often submit their newer clients for MOS spots with the belief that they are easier and a good place for actors to get their feet wet.

Quite the contrary! MOS auditions can be very challenging for any actor, new *or* experienced.

Often there's no script in the lobby for you to use as fodder to start stimulating your brain. You may not have any idea what will be asked of you until you walk into the audition.

Sometimes casting directors will post the basic scenario, or they may come out to the lobby and give all the actors an explanation. The session director may bring a large group into the studio for a group explanation. And sometimes they won't do a thing.

I always advise my students to catch an actor who has just auditioned and is on the way out the door; ask, "So how did it go? What did they have you do?"

Actors love to talk (and they love to talk about themselves!), so usually you will get something.

Even if the actor says, "Oh, it is really easy; you're just in an elevator,"

you'll have something to begin to work on. You can use this nugget of information to ask yourself some questions and make some choices.

First ask yourself, *What do I want?* This is the objective in the scene.

Then ask yourself, *How do I get that?* This is the action in the scene.

So if we start with the information that you are in an elevator, *What do I want?* To get to the office on time. To go see my boyfriend after work or perhaps visit a loved one in the hospital.

How do I get that accomplished? Wait for the door to open.

I always ask myself, *How do I feel?* or *What is my point of view?* This is a tremendous help in making me stand out from the rest in a positive way, one that serves the scene. Am I relaxed because I know the boss is on vacation? Am I tense because he warned me three times about being late to work? Now I have something happening internally.

I find it is always best to use experiences that I have encountered myself, something that just happened in the last week or two if at all possible. This keeps it fresh and still in my body. In this way I can picture my surroundings and the situation.

Avoid making up situations that you have never had, because you will have a much more difficult time making it real for yourself.

Though we don't speak words in a MOS spot, it doesn't mean words shouldn't fill our head and our thoughts— about what we want, how to get it, and how we feel in the moment.

In the elevator scene, for example, you have built in an inner monologue that is going on the whole time you're standing there with the doors closed:

Why did I wear this blouse, my boyfriend hates this blouse, I am hungry, why didn't I eat breakfast, maybe I can sneak out and grab one of those delicious carrot muffins from the coffee shop, did I bring money? Shoot! Maybe I

can borrow a few bucks from Bill . . . he likes me . . . etc.,
etc., all while you stand quietly in the elevator. Trust that
just having this inner monologue will hold and ground you
in the scene.

My motto is *know, don't show!* You don't have to show
us you're thinking these thoughts. Just think them. This
insures your performance will be real and motivated, and
it will be clear that you are in action with motivation and
a point of view. Your inner thoughts keep you engaged in
the scene, and you will always stand out because of your
commitment to the moment.

**You get noticed because you are 100% committed to
your objective and engaged in your activity—not because
you do some bizarre outrageous action.**

When my students do the MOS elevator exercise in
class, most actors try to do too much and work at it too
hard. For instance, to show that they really have to go to
the bathroom, they cross their legs, jump up and down,
wince and squirm.

Instead, they should just have thoughts and an inner
monologue, *"I really shouldn't have had that coffee! It went
right through me. I won't even have time to go to my desk; I
will just go right to the bathroom. Oh darn, I have this jump-
suit on; why didn't I wear the jeans I laid out? Tomorrow I
will wear them, oh, with that new cute top I bought . . . did
I wash that?"* . . . and so forth.

Feel free to use a prop for the audition, though it should

be something that you would realistically have with you in the elevator—a phone, purse, briefcase, notepad—anything that would be appropriate to the circumstances. Stella Adler, the famous actor and acting teacher, said, "The prop will keep you truthful."

Chapter 6

The Spokesperson Audition—Just You

Without wonder and insight, acting is just a business.
With it, it becomes creation.
—Bette Davis, actor

Spokesperson is a pretty dated term, but it's still used for commercial spots when only one person talks to the camera. The style has evolved over the years, though. Spokesperson commercials used to be more presentational in their approach, but nowadays the spots are more matter of fact in both the delivery and the style.

The actor's goals for this type of commercial are first to make sense of the material, and then to make it sound as natural as possible

Though you're the only person talking in a spokesperson audition, let go of the idea that it is a monologue. Instead, you should think of it as a dialogue between you and another person whose comments can't be heard.

First calls are usually quite relaxed—generally they're just you and the session director. In the first call, all questions and rehearsals are only seen and heard by the session director; he is there to get you to your best performance and send that take to the director.

Session directors want you to be great! However, they can't afford to spend a ton of time to help you get there. You do need to be prepared and have choices. This is your chance to ask questions: *What is the style and tone of the piece? Is there room for comedy?* Get as much info from the session director as you can up front, and process it in your body before you begin.

The following pages contain two script examples:

This is a Straightforward interview... Documentary Style spot

Hero is Standing by a copier in Punk rock makeup and costume

I don't know why they say it. I was just doing my job. They couldn't leave the computers, flip charts and binders, so I suggested they go to Supply Warehouse and pick up those cool flash drives and put the presentation on those. Next thing I know, I am the office rock star. No... I like country music.

Now let's break it down and show how to make this a *dialogue* and not a *monologue*. We will fill in the responses your imaginary scene partner might say in between your lines. You will have a cue card. Make your cue card part of the fourth wall.

Where are you? Let's say you are at the office. Know what you can look at in the office so you can justify looking at the cue card in a natural way. A good place to be is the break room getting coffee. Your co-worker (now both your cue card and the object of a secret little crush you have) just asked you,

"How come everyone is calling you a rock star?"
You answer with your first line:

Yeah, I don't know why. I was just doing my job.
Notice I added the "*Yeah,*" in response to his question.

Then your co-worker says, "**Really?**" and you respond:

Well, they couldn't leave the computers, flip charts and binders, so I suggested they go to Supply Warehouse and pick up those cool flash drives and put the presentation on those.

Now you're motivated to defend yourself and what you did.

Your co-worker then asks, *"So what happened?"*
And you say: *Next thing I know, I am the office rock star.*

They might ask, *"Are you?"* to which you respond the final scripted line: *Nooo... I like country music.*

I always like to add a button. Here are some examples:

- Or jazz.
- Really!
- Tammy Wynette! (or Earl Scruggs, Dolly Parton)
- I listen in the car.

The button can be any number of things that are short and simple, no more than three words. Buttons add my own personality and are memorable in a way that serves the scene. I button all the time.

Every take, I do a different button. The more a button sounds like the next natural thing you would say, the better. *Avoid selling,* as it is not your job.

Your job is to play the scene. The advertiser's job is to sell. **Never** add *Try it, you'll like it,* or *It is delicious!*

The simpler, the better!

Commercial auditions are about carving out a personal moment where you are really talking to someone and really have a need for that.

When you start out, it may be helpful to use the cue card as the person you are talking to. As you become more comfortable doing spokesperson auditions, you really want to use the camera and speak directly to it.

Put someone very specific right in the lens, someone that you talk to on a regular basis, because you know how you talk to them. This will ground you.

Try your hand at being a spokesperson with this copy.

Community Banks of Colorado – "Hard At Work"

Open on a bank employee sitting behind his desk and staring at his computer intently. He looks up at the camera.

Bank employee:
"Common sense dictates that if you're up front with your customers then they're more likely to want to grow a long-term relationship with you. Here at Community Banks of Colorado everything we do is based on straightforward talk and transparency. So in the interest of full disclosure you should know that I'm actually watching a golf match right now.

He turns his computer around to the camera and we see golf on his computer.

Titles:
No hidden fees.
No hidden disclosures.
Simple, honest talk.

Logo and tagline:
Community Banks of Colorado.
Where Common Sense Lives.

Chapter 7

Commercial Scenes— Auditioning With Another Actor

Count on only one person, the person who you know 100% will be there
with you when you draw your last breath of life.
That person you must count on is you!
—Stuart J. Scesney, agent, casting director, and author

You check your email, and you have an audition tomorrow. Fantastic!

You look through the audition info and find the copy. Oh, boy! It is a nice scene, something you can really work on.

A scene is one of the toughest auditions you can do. Scene auditions involve reading cue cards, handling props, moving physically in relation to a partner, creating character choices and maintaining an inner life. All these elements must be handled without much—if any!—rehearsal.

The good thing about doing scenes is you get to work with another actor.

The bad thing about doing scenes is that you have to work with another actor.

The scene can go either way.

It can be brilliant, chemistry flying, you're a match made in heaven and the two of you have all kinds of knock-em-dead moments all over the audition room. You leave, full of confidence, and say happily, "See ya on the set!" Yes, you can definitely have those scene auditions, and you feel on top of the world—you knocked it out of the park.

But you can't count on that happening. More times than not, your partner will not be as prepared as you, he won't even look at you, he will be fifteen years your senior, and you won't be able get anything from this guy!

You can *still* get a callback and/or book the job if you do your part.

First of all, *don't* expect anything from your scene partner. Don't expect him to give you the cues, the right lines, or even anything to play off. Your partner's success is not contingent upon you or your success. You also need to realize that your partner is not responsible for your getting a callback.

Your performance and choices are *your* responsibility. So play the scene, make your choices based on what you are getting, and let the session director handle your partner. Believe me, directors know what to do with him better than you will. When the audition is over, you'll look like a true professional. The director may even feel like you should have another chance with a different actor.

As an actor, you will make a terrible trap for yourself if you tell the other actor how you are going to play it or what to do. This is a sure-fire way to disaster.
First of all, *it is not your job.*

Second, in everyday life, we don't tell those around us how we are going to behave in the next few moments. Why would you do it before your scene?

Third, never forget that most actors—me included— never respond well to another actor telling them how to play the scene.

So instead, **play the scene.** I probably say that 20 times a night when we work on scenes in class.

My twelve-step program for working a successful scene will insure your performance is rich, full, and noticeable.

1. Choose the relationship

Find the innate relationship between you and your partner. Is it brother/sister, mom/daughter, boss/employee, class-mates? Perhaps more esoteric?

Sometimes these relationships are provided in the script or by the session director, and more often they're not. Even the basic relationships stated in a script don't come with much acting gasoline, though. For example, say the director says your relationship with your partner is co-worker. You can't have the same relationship with every co-worker; some you might be really playful with, and some you would like to avoid. So, be specific; infuse the relationship with some qualifiers such as *overbearing supervisor, incompetent intern* or *sexy salesman*. Make your partner a person who activates something in you to facilitate the scene.

Have a couple of backup relationships in mind so you're not locked into doing it one way. Scenes require you to be flexible and not rigid in your choices.

2. Find a contrast in the relationship

Contrast creates instant chemistry/conflict, and this is desirable in a scene. Good scenes have conflict built in. Sometimes you will have to find the contrast or infuse a little into the character so it gives you a more active choice. Here are some classic contrasts which always work and can be found in many commercial scenes:

- High-strung/mellow (anxious shopper and apathetic clerk)
- Stupid/smart (loveable loser husband and savvy wife)
- Neatnik/slob (anal-compulsive mother and teen slacker)
- Chintzy/spendthrift (overly cheap boss with extravagant salesman)

3. Know how you feel about the other character.

Have a point of view for this moment in time. Yes, your

scene partner might be your husband whom you love dearly, but you have told him for the last two weeks that the house needed painting and he has to go to the hardware store. Right now, your point of view may be irritation, frustration and wanting the house to be painted already. It doesn't mean you should yell at him, but choosing the point of view that you have told him the line 20 times already as opposed to this being the first time will make for very different takes.

4. Listen and react naturally

It is staggering how often we actors do not listen to what our partner says to us. We are so busy worrying about how we are going to cleverly deliver our next line that we miss an opportunity to have a natural reaction, which will motivate our line much better than how we rehearsed it in our heads.

Do not indicate your reaction. Just listen and have your point of view so we know what you are thinking. The practice of active listening gives you real, subtle reactions. **Know, don't show** is my favorite motto.

5. Play the beginning, middle, and end of the scene

Yes, all of that is included in a three-second spot. It is your job to establish what happened right before the scene starts, what the climax of the scene or turning point is, and what is the resolve and how to keep the life going after the last scripted line. This is necessary to do for yourself, even if your only line is a response to, "Do you want fries with that?"

The beginning of the scene is fueled by where you just came from or what you just heard. Your first scripted line is always generated by something that preceded it; the scene doesn't start in a vacuum. Don't expect this information will be given to you. Some savvy session directors will give you something, but remember they will probably give the same info to every actor who auditions for the role. Do you want to do the same thing on the audition tape that every other actor does?

I caution you not to make it some grandiose, extraordinary happening. Keep it real and within the scope of your life and your role. Make it something that would naturally occur before you order a hamburger. Perhaps you checked your wallet to make sure your credit card is in there. Or perhaps a friend called and asked you to bring a burger back to the office.

The middle or the climax/turn of the scene is just that. What changes?

Look for the change and then you can construct the rise to the turn of the scene. The bigger the stakes, the bigger the turn. So make sure you want something enough, even if it is just to order a hamburger.

The end of the scene should have a wrap up, a *button* as I like to call it, which keeps the life going for yourself and finishes the scene with a real end. I always add a word or two to three to *tag* the scene after the last scripted line when it is appropriate. If I don't add a button, I still keep the life going, knowing what I want and keeping the scene alive until I hear cut!

6. Pace

There are not a lot of pauses in commercial scenes; they're wasted time. Pace doesn't mean you race through the lines, it means you pick up the cues, as we do in life. In our everyday conversations, we practically finish each other's sentences. This practice will help you tremendously in scenes.

When there is a pause, fill it—the scene will have more natural energy and excitement with some built-in urgency. If your partner doesn't give you the right cue line, fill in the blanks with whatever cue you need to get your own line out.

7. It's critical that you use the fourth wall

I have an audition rule: Motivate to your partner 25% of the time, and out to the fourth wall 75% of the time.

Auditions use a stationary camera, which makes it a very different setup from the actual shoots. When you have an audition with another person, generally the camera becomes part of the fourth wall. Your job as actor becomes compounded: Play the scene out enough so the camera, the director and the client are able to see your reactions.

The temptation is always to turn and face your partner, and talk to just him. In an audition scene, this is death for an actor. You simply will *not* be seen. Avoiding this trap takes practice and awareness, and unfortunately you will often be told by session directors to *cheat out*, putting your body in an awkward position, facing the fourth wall and turning to talk to your partner.

I prefer to *motivate out*. Instead of cheating out, you need to find a motivation to look at the fourth wall most of the time. This involves practice, practice, and more practice.

Motivating to the fourth wall is unique to the audition and only used then. The fourth wall is the focus to which you must play most of the action, *without* looking at the camera itself. Ask yourself, "What do I see?" Find one or two things that would make sense for you to gaze at on the fourth wall and give yourself reasons to look at them. I find that if I practice having my feet facing the camera, I will be in a good position for the scene.

8. Buttons are very important

In a scene I am often asked, "Who buttons? The person with the last line or the person without the final line?" Don't expect your partner to button. Have one ready. If we have done our homework, we as actors should know the next thing we would say in this situation.

I come up with a few possibilities, and then I make sure

I shorten the phrases to three words or less. It's important that they're all ready to go; I let the moment with my partner dictate which one I actually say.

One very foolproof way to find out what you would say after the last scripted line is to do some individual brainstorming, as I call it. Brainstorming is writing down all the things I would see or hear in a given environment.

For example, let's say the scene take place at a dinner party. Ask yourself, "What would I see at this dinner party?" Your brain pictures a beautiful table, hors d'hoeuvres, cocktails, crab puffs, patio, candles, flower arrangements, bathroom, napkins, etc.

Now ask what you might hear being said by your fellow guests at this dinner party. Your brain fills with: Delicious dinner, what's for dessert, lovely table, can I help? Who made the salad? Who's Marty with? Are you going to finish that?

Now I have actually filled my brain with many choices for banter and buttons I can use that make sense in the scene. The more natural the button is, the funnier it is. Try brainstorming at every audition, and you will make great use of the waiting time

9. Prepare the scene two different ways

Always be ready with another way to go; you cannot afford to get locked into just one way of doing a scene. Your partner may be headed in another direction, and it will be easier for you to jump on his train if you have explored other options for the scene. It will also be easier when you are asked to do the scene a second time; you'll have something different to add in the second take.

We are *actors*; we need to have many different ways to go with a scene. Preparing different approaches is also excellent practice for shooting a job where they always throw new things or new lines at you—you have to stay flexible. Directors always need actors to repeat a performance, and they need the actor to bring fresh and innovative takes during a long day on the set.

10. Keep your inner life going on, especially when it is not your line

This goes back to listening to the other actor. It's your job to know what you should be thinking while you are listening. Write down a few simple inner thoughts that should be going through your head while the other actor is talking. Rehearse these like you would dialogue. Don't cut yourself off from new thoughts, though; leave yourself open to other things coming in as well.

Make sure you know how you feel and keep these based in reality. The more real it is, the easier it will be for you to stay in the scene and steal the scene just by your reactions.

11. Have an activity

Ah, activities! The simple act of doing something physical is very powerful. It grounds the actor, and the director sees real behavior. Finding an activity that is appropriate to the scene can be tricky, but don't overthink it. Choose a simple yet specific activity suitable to the given circumstances.

The activity shouldn't dominate you, but rather, it should give you purpose in the scene and make the actions personal and unique to you.

Don't just stand there talking about the groceries— unpack them while you listen and talk! Unpack them the way you always do. This calls for you to be self-aware. You'll need some practice and the ability to use recall in your daily life; it's a necessary part of acting.

Start being more and more self-aware of the way you do things and how you handle props. Activities can give an actor a leg up in being more natural and real in the scene. Sometimes I have an actor do a simple thing like take a jacket off or put one on during the scene just to give them something to focus on other than the words.

12. *Always* ask for a rehearsal

When you have a scene partner for an audition, you want to know what they are going to give you (or not) before your first take. The session director can see what is going on, and she may offer some direction to the scene. You usually get only two takes, rarely a third for time reasons—so this is actually a chance to get one more take. If you wait for the session director to ask *you* if you want a rehearsal, your ego will answer despite yourself, "No, let's just tape one."

It is always better to rehearse first, so be bold and ask for a rehearsal. This is not a sign of a beginner--it is a sign of a professional actor, and it's also a free chance for you to see what and who you are going to be working with.

Before you enter the audition room, you should make as many choices as you can about who you are in the scene, what you want, and how you are going to do it. However, do not do line readings. If you wish to run lines for cues, that is fine, but know it is not about the words. The only lines that are critical are those lines where the product is being described or mentioned.

It is much more important to play the scene and explore the relationship. Respond to and work off of your partner as much as his or her talent will allow. At the same time, never abandon what you know you must do to make the scene work. Always remember that you should enjoy this. After all, you have been given an opportunity to act!

Chapter 8

Stick to the Script . . . or Make it Your Own?
Improvisation for Commercial Auditions

*I love improvisation. You can't blame it on the writers. You can't blame it
on direction. You can't blame it on the camera guy . . . it's you. You're on.
You've got to do it, and you either sink or swim with what you've got.*
—Jonathan Winters, actor, comedian, artist, author

Improvisation is the art or act of inventing, composing,
executing, or arranging something without previous prepa-
ration. Improvisation is also a skill that can be developed
with training.

***Improv is the number one skill set casting directors
look for when choosing actors for comedic commercial
spots.*** Most commercial breakdowns even stress, "Must

have improv chops."

Don't be intimidated! When you think about it, we all improvise every day because we don't use scripted lines when we talk to our loved ones or the barista at Starbucks. We are improvising all the time without even knowing it. With improv training under your belt, though, you feel freedom and confidence, and the training allows you to let go.

Improv skills are a major asset in doing better at auditions. Many auditions today have no dialogue and require improv skills, so agents are encouraging their clients to take improvisation classes to make them more marketable and get more auditions.

When actors don't book a commercial, their agent may say the comforting words that actors have heard since the beginning of time, "They just went another way," and sometimes that may even be true. Many casting offices have told me, though, that the reason an actor didn't book was because he didn't take a chance; he performed exactly what was on the page rather than adding a little unscripted something to the audition. He didn't add his own unique stamp.

I used to say, "I am going to leave them with a little bit of Judy." My improv, added to their commercial copy, could often equal a booking.

My audition for Direct TV is a good example. I played a mom who calls the plumbers to fix my sink, and when I have to run out, I leave the guys there to do their job. The plumbers see the Direct TV Satellite on the roof and end up sitting around drinking beer and eating popcorn while watching TV. When my character comes back, I don't have a scripted line—I am just supposed to react. I decided to come in and catch them in the act in my living room. I plopped my purse down to get their attention and said, "COMFY?" Though the audition room had been very cool and aloof up to that point, it just busted up laughing as the tension was broken. I booked that job and my "Comfy?" was added to the script.

Another example is a series of spots I booked for Starz Network. I played a switchboard operator who dispatched super heroes to save the day. It was just me talking on the phone, so it was critical that I knew what the caller was saying on the other end. Knowing the caller's dialogue gave me the freedom to put my own spin on the spot and add little ad libs, improvising what I did and what I said on the phone to the callers. In one spot, I chose to file my nails with my feet up on the counter while I took a call from a screaming woman in distress. I added a casual comment after the call ended, "Nice gal . . . great set of pipes." It got a great response from everyone in the room at the callback, and I ended up booking the series. They used my tag in the spot as well.

"Although we can't ask anyone to improvise [because of Screen Actors Guild rules], people will expect you to be able to," says David Cady, a session director with Donna

DeSeta's office in New York. "At the very least, people will appreciate that you can make a funny script funnier."

"Ultimately, you have to find a way to make your audition stand out from everyone else's," observes Cady, who has personally cast more than 1,500 commercials in the last decade. "Improv may be the way to do it."

It is true. Legally, SAG-AFTRA does not allow actors to improvise dialogue at their auditions, so actors are never officially asked to improvise. However, the casting offices will often suggest that the actors "feel free to go off script," "make it your own," "have fun with it." These are all code words for *Please improvise!*

Standard acting training focuses on the specific techniques of motivation, emotional connection, subtext, and character development. Good improvisational training instead focuses on creativity, commitment, listening, trusting your instincts, and supporting the other actor. It frees you up and allows you to express within the confines of the scene.

Don't worry if you are not known for being funny, or if you don't feel creative or instinctive. A good improv teacher doesn't focus on humor. When you are "in the moment," when you're not thinking or planning but just following your instincts, you will find that you are actually creative and often quite funny. Improv is about freedom, and it is a process that is achieved in a safe space with a teacher who creates a supportive and noncompetitive environment.

Though many studios mix in the improv training with acting, commercial, and cold reading, it's best to learn the basic improv games and exercises in a class that focuses only on improvisation.

I strongly believe that improvisation should be a second training workshop along with your acting class; it can be done in tandem with your technique classes. When you study both acting and improv at the same time, you will get the maximum out of your acting class and be ready to start auditioning sooner.

Improvisation is a must-have tool in your actor's kit.

Chapter 9

The Fallbacks of Callbacks

I've come to believe that everything worth achieving is beyond one's capacity—or seems so at first. The thing is to persist, not back off, fight your fight, pay your dues, and carry on. Effort is all; continue and you may get there despite everything!
—Elia Kazan, director, producer, actor, screenwriter, novelist, acting teacher

You have a *callback* when the director requests you to come back and audition again—and this time it's in front of the creative team. In Los Angeles, callbacks are often referred to as *allbacks* because it seems as if the director hasn't narrowed down the selection at all—perhaps he even called in some new actors to see if anyone in LA hadn't already been considered for this particular job.

It can be frustrating, but my sage advice is that you rise above it. Never show even the smallest hint of your frustration. Instead, be grateful. Have gratitude that you were selected to return; now you have a chance for some face time with the director and client. The callback is your opportunity to turn their heads and get picked for the job.

Another term for the callback is the *fallback*, for it is full of unexpected elements and factors completely beyond your control. The script may have changed; the concept may be completely different from your first audition. They may even have you read for another role you didn't even know about.

Don't panic!

My callback credo is to always show up with the expectation that things *will* be different. You can jump up and down the rare times that everything is unchanged from your first call.

The very first thing you want to do is sign in, then find a quiet place to sit. I make a point to avoid the chit chat; there are too many chances to come unglued or psyched out. One actress always talks to those she views as her competition, and she does her best to get the upper hand. Once she told me how she had just booked something and wasn't sure if it would be a conflict for this job—a classic psych for an actor. Another time, just as I was called, she told me I had a little spot on my shirt. She pretended to try and rub it out, and said, "Oh, they will never notice!" Of course there was no spot, but believe me, I thought about that spot all the way down the hall.

Socialize *after* your audition. Use this time to get centered and become confident in your choices. Be grateful for being called back.

Be ready for anything, give whatever happens 110% of your focus and attention, and keep your ears open to hear the direction.

Walking in to the room when you're called is an art form. You must be confident, not cocky; self-sufficient, not needy; ready and prepared, not anxious or flustered.

Leave everything outside the room including coats, umbrellas, and emotional baggage. Walk in unencumbered, free and ready to play!

From this moment forward, banish these nagging internal questions forever: ***"What do they want?" "What are they looking for?"***

You—*the actor*—are the one who brings in a solid choice within the realm of what is appropriate for the scene. You are the one who makes it your own and commits to that choice. Your vision for the role is what turns the director's head.

The minute you worry about the illusive *they* and what *they* want, you give your power away to the room. I always tell actors, "Walk in the room believing you have the job."

This means you must have the attitude that the call you received was really to book the job, and this is an informal meeting with the director. This attitude positively affects the way you behave in the callback room.

Directors often get their inspiration from you! Your vision of the role might stimulate them to give you a *note,* or redirection. This is a good thing! It means you are giving them something to play with.

The last thing a director wants is have to pull a performance out of an actor. It is exhausting. Directors are happy as clams when you deliver, take after take, keeping it fresh and new but hitting the beats each time. This is what directors look for.

When a director gives you a note, listen and say out loud in your own words what you think you heard him say. For example, if the director says, "Try it again, and this time, don't pause at the end," you might respond with, "Great, so at the end just keep my life going?"

Then they might say, "No, I want you to take the beat, just quicker." And you'll paraphrase, "Great, so reaction quicker at the end?"

When you paraphrase the direction, you have the opportunity to use that moment to process the note and let it go into your body. You will also remember the note more by saying it out loud rather than just nodding and saying, "Got it!"

Often we *think* we are listening, but nothing is being absorbed when our nerves are blocking our receptors.

Your attitude and personality are being auditioned as well as your talent. The director and creative team want to see how you will be on the set *all day long.* The easier you are to work with, the more you can listen and deliver to the best of your ability what they are asking, the better.

A good poker face is handy to have at callbacks. You never want to leave the room showing them you did not have the winning hand. Stay pleasant and thankful until you get back to your car.

You probably did better than you think. Even if you didn't, there is always another audition.

Practice, practice, practice is the key. Go to workout groups. Practice copy in front of people and think of yourself as a booker! Practice until you truly are one.

Nothing looks better on an actor than the glow of just having booked a job!

Chapter 10

Your Castable Self

Acting is not about being someone different. It's finding the similarity in what is apparent different, then finding myself in there.
—Meryl Streep, actor

If you don't know who you can be in commercials, how is anyone else going to know? If you don't know who you *are*, how will you ever get an audition, or even dream of booking a commercial?

Most commercials are 30 seconds long, and the actors' actual screen time can be seconds. The visual story you tell as a person is instantaneous. Those few seconds are all you have. This is why you need to answer the question, **What is my castable self?**

Your *castable self* is what you look like to people at first glance. It may have very little to do with who you are as a person. This is where most people have a difficult time. An actor may project decisiveness and success like a powerful

CEO type, but he's really a dropout who lives on a friend's boat. An actress may appear to be an uptight, prudish librarian, but watch out for her wild side (and she strips on the side, too).

This is where honest self-appraisal and the help of a great coach will serve you well.

A good commercial acting class often helps you discover your castable self. I always include this as part of the course for my commercial classes. It is vital to send actors out to the world of auditions armed with the knowledge of **who they are** and **who they will be cast as.**

You can ask yourself some questions and work through the process. First start with:

What's your age range? This is how old you *appear*, not your real age. Give yourself a five-year to seven-year range. Any more than seven years is not realistic.

What type are you? Upper class/middle class/ or lower/blue collar? Rural or urban? Southern or craggy New

Englander? Ex-football player, or nerdy/pasty video gamer?

What jobs might you have? Office worker or CEO? Multi-tasking mom or the mom who cannot get her kids lunches together without a mishap? Waitress or construction worker?

What is your essence? This always gets a quizzical look. *Essence* is your personality. Are you dry, smug, perky, chatty, judgmental, earnest, eager, helpful, frazzled, organized, calm, energetic?

Let's say you're 18-25. Let's analyze what jobs you might have:
- Senior in high school
- College student
- Barista
- Counter girl/guy at a fast food restaurant
- Office clerk
- Retail clerk
- Intern at an office
- Bike messenger
- Hipster
- Troubled teen
- Sorority girl
- Soldier/sailor/marine

Now add status and your essence:
- Valedictorian in high school or the kid in alternative school
- Rich Ivy League college student or junior college

commuter student
- Edgy barista or chatty barista
- Helpful counter girl/guy at a fast food restaurant or slacker
- Eager office clerk or bored office clerk
- Smug retail clerk or chatty retail clerk
- Earnest intern in an office or the boss's cocky son
- Lazy bike messenger or super jock racing bike messenger
- Trendy, edgy vibe hipster on Melrose or from Brooklyn
- Behind in studies teen or joined a gang teen
- Comes from money and privilege coed or "just here to party" girl.
- Navy SEAL or Air Force mechanic

Do you get the idea? We need to be specific and honest with ourselves on how we come off. We need to know the role in which we will most likely be cast.

It does not end here. Now you must make a list of the individuals in your life who bring out different qualities in you.

- Who makes you feel competitive?
- Who are you completely honest with?
- Who always makes you feel flirty and sexy?
- Who brings out that edgy side? Is it your best friend when you're out at a club on Saturday night? What does he or she say to you?
- If you are the earnest intern in the office, who brings out your desire to please?

As an actor, you need to recreate a scene in your life, so put those people in the camera lens when you shoot your headshots. They will ensure that your authentic essence is captured in your eyes and hints at your status and essence. This is even more important than the clothes you select.

Start to look at yourself the way the industry sees you

Tom Burke, an image consultant, refers to actors' clothing as the uniform. Every type, every category, every marketable role has a certain uniform way of dressing that speaks to the viewer and eliminates the need for unnecessary exposition. Not only can the right clothes play a part in booking a job, more importantly, the wrong clothes can lose a job for an actor as well.

Think about it—acting uses a visual medium. When the camera cuts to a character, whether in a television show, a movie, or especially a commercial, the audience immediately have a sense of who the character is and what his role is just by the way he looks—his type, his age, and the clothes he wears.

The same is true for any actor walking into an audition or a meeting. A casting director, director, agent or manager must be able to look at you or your headshot and know instantly who you are and how and where you fit in.

Your job as an actor is to study television, movies, and commercials, not only for the current acting styles and trends, but also for the current clothing, hair style, and makeup trends (women only, please!) for your specific type and categories.

If you truly want to be castable, you need to know who you are and what you have to offer. If you want to get on the field and play with the big guys, you must wear the uniform. Clothes really can play a part in booking a job.

Costumes

My suggestion is that you build a small wardrobe of *costumes* —tried and true outfits for castable roles you are right for and will be called in for. Make sure they are always clean and ready to go, so when you have a call for a high-powered business woman, you can pull out your blue suit and scarf and throw them in the car. Bring those pumps too; they will make you feel like a high-powered business woman the minute you squeeze your tootsies into them.

Have at least four good selections to choose from for your *nice casual* costume, based on the research you have done on who you are. I have two different outfits for my nice casual look. For a more middle- to lower-class or at-home nice casual look, I wear a Gap button-down shirt with a small floral print, with either a modest camisole or a sweater. I would never wear this outfit in my daily life because it is not my style, but it gets me in the right mood and has actually been in several commercials, so I know it works.

My other nice casual outfit is a bit more Beverly Hills-casual, a little brighter, and it looks a little more pulled together.

The two suits that I wear for business executive roles came from Goodwill for under $20.00 each, and they've both been used in commercials multiple times. I mix them up with a scarf or a set of pearls, but they are my only two choices when I get the call for an executive role. If your costume works, don't change it!

You want to have a good costume that makes you feel the part, that looks good on you, and most definitely that looks good on camera. If you have questions, ask a professional image consultant. The investment is worth it in the long run, and it will make your life so much easier on a daily basis.

Tom Burke and Buckley Sampson are two excellent image consultants whom I've recommended to many students.

Chapter 11

Headshots

The truth of ourselves is the root of our acting.
—Sanford Meisner

All novice actors are told, "You need headshots to get started!"

So they choose some outfits: a blazer for the business look, something good-looking for nice casual, and of course a sexy outfit they love. They find any decent photographer that they can afford, and they spend their money getting shots that make them look more glamorous than they have ever looked before, with way too much makeup on and hair styled by a pro in a way they will never be able to duplicate in a million years.

They get the pictures touched up, erasing every wrinkle and tell-tale sign of their uniqueness out of the shot. They print up the headshots in mass quantities and start sending them out.

You, however, are ahead of the game because you've done the self-appraisal in the previous chapter. You are now ready to find a really good photographer to showcase your unique, castable self.

Choose the right photographer

Research: Do your due diligence with photographers. Their websites are helpful, but they're not always an accurate way to find out how a photographer works. It is best to ask other actors, so you can look at the actor in person and compare with the headshot to see if the photographer captured the brand of the actor.

Lighting is important. Your headshot has to be professionally lit to show up well online. Check headshots for good lighting and see if the actors' eyes have life in them.

Check the backgrounds that the photographer uses. A background can make all the difference in a shot. If you have dark brown hair, a black background will make you blend in; we won't know where you begin and the background ends. You don't want a tree growing out of your head, either, or a bright yellow background if you're pale and blonde.

The background should allow you to pop. We want to see you!

Cost: The more you pay doesn't mean the better the shot will be, but your friend with her phone is not a great option, either. You should be able to get great shots for under $400.

Meet the photographer first: Talk to the photographers and see if you are comfortable with them before you make a decision and commit. You will need to trust them, open up and show various sides of yourself, so you better be comfortable or it will show in your shots.

Hair and makeup: Many photographers offer hair and makeup for an additional charge, but I strongly urge you to do your own. When makeup and hair are done by a stranger, you don't look like yourself. Invariably, you end up looking too glamorous. Worse, you'll be unable to recreate your look when you audition. Strive for looking like yourself on a good day. Keep your makeup and hair natural, not perfect.

Clothes: Know what you want to wear for the shoot, and have a couple other options as well. Get a professional opinion on your wardrobe; actors are not that good at picking outfits for shoots. Your uniform should *suggest* a character, not dominate or overpower you. Only the neck and shoulders of an outfit will show, so pick wisely.

Here is what Valencia, one of my students, said after meeting with Tom Burke prior to her photo shoot:

"The tools and tips he gave me for taking charge in front of the camera will be useful for many, many years to come. As a result of all our combined efforts, my headshots make the connection we were seeking, that connection revealed the most amazingly artful, animated, and fresh photos!"

Picking the shot: After the shoot, hire a professional to help you pick your shot. It is best to get an opinion from an active casting director or headshot coach. You should never decide on the shot you are going to use. I know that sounds crazy, but rarely can an actor be objective enough to pick a winning shot. Actors always wants the shot where they look gorgeous, and that is not the goal. Instead, print the pretty one and frame it for your mantle at home.

For commercials, you want a shot that shows who you are, your essence and a little secret behind the eyes. This is your castable self.

Casting director Ross Lacy told me, "The kiss of death is when an actor comes into my office. If I see your picture and I say, 'Oh my god, this person is perfect,' I am going to give you one of these valuable 100 slots. Then you come in, and I am like, 'Who is this person? This is not *that* person! That is not this person at all!' That stands out in my mind more than anything, because I have wasted time.

"The headshot should be an accurate representation of not only what you look like, but of whom you are!

"The days of the big smiley commercial shots are gone. It shouldn't feel like you're trying too hard. Remember, too, that pictures can't be *too* perfect--makeup too perfect, hair too perfect. It comes off overdone, as though you're trying too hard. I much prefer natural. Your hair should be like it would be if you come in here.

"The pictures are not for the agents. They are for **us**. For casting."

Retouching

Once you get your shots and you have selected four or five to use, resist the urge to ask the photographer to retouch them. Retouching is like candy or potato chips, you can't stop after just one. The photo should look like you today, not ten years ago. So leave the lines around the eyes. Leave the furrows on the brow. If you have a mole and we can see it, leave it!

Retouching should be only to remove a stray hair or temporary pimple. Everything else should stay. The photo needs to look like you today and like you will look when you walk into the audition. If you need retouching, remember that less is more!

Printing the headshot

Headshots are not used in mass quantities as they once were. Actors used to order prints of 300 headshots on a regular basis; their agents had to send out hard copies to casting for every job submission. Now everything is done online, and your photos are easily accessible to review for submissions.

Fortunately, printing costs are minimal for actors. You do want a high-resolution print of every shot that you'll use to upload to each online casting site. Don't use a low-resolution jpg; high-rez digital image has more clarity and will make a big difference when your headshot is viewed online.

- Be sure to Crop just below the neck or collar bone for most online sites.
- Print at least 25 copies of your headshot; keep them in your car at all times just in case they are needed.
- Make sure you print your name on the front of your headshots. The prints can easily separate from your résumé, and if they like your headshot, they won't be able to identify you. Include your own contact number on the résumé so you can be reached when your agency is closed.

Uploading your headshot

Beau Brians

Once you select several shots that will give casting an accurate view of who you are, upload the high-resolution photo onto the sites. A low-resolution version of the shot will looks fuzzy and won't pop on the small screen. Make sure it is clear, color-corrected and ready to load. Here are must-use sites:

- LA Casting
- Actors Access
- IMDB
- Casting Frontier
- LinkedIn
- Facebook
- Google

Eljae Brown

The ones listed above are a must, though I suggest you post your picture on any legitimate site you can access. To broaden your reach, make sure you include a profile with the photos wherever you can.

You want to be selective about the photos you load. More photos per site don't make your outreach better; less is more. Have three to five different looks at the most, and make sure they all look like you are right now. If they all have the same smile and same outfit, narrow it down to one shot per outfit.

Griffin Kunitz

You want to give the viewer a sneak peek into who you are and who you could be cast as. Be

Eric Satterberg

97

realistic and honest with yourself about your marketability.

Actors are cursed with the myth that they can do anything. First you have to establish yourself as a talent with strength before you expand your career. Charlize Theron starred in a dozen films as the hot, beautiful, girl who broke men's hearts. Only after establishing her name and talent was she able to be taken seriously for the serial killer role in *Monster* that won her an Academy Award. She never would have been able to even read for it before she established herself.

Headshots are the actor's #1 marketing tool

Make sure you're not one of the many actors who send out or post generic shots that look good but say absolutely nothing about their type, brand, or marketability.

Take charge of your session and make it worth every bit of the time, energy and money you put into it.

Résumé

Your résumé presents your background and skills to a prospective employer. Even though most actors' résumés are posted online at sites used by casting and producers/directors, you need to keep a printed copy on hand at *all times*. On page 101 check out the example that we've included in order to show you a recommended style.

Here's more detail about what should be on an actor's résumé:

- **Name.** This should be the first thing the eye goes to; typically, it's centered. Make sure it's bold and in a prominent position.
- **Union affiliations**. List all you're involved in.
- **Agency representation.** Most agents have a logo; use it, as the branding is helpful. Always list *all* your representation.
- **Physical stats**: Your height/weight/eye/hair color. Just keep it current.
- **Contact info**: Your cell phone for when your agency is closed. A job may be lost if the agent is not available or they can't reach you. If you or your agent can't be reached, they move on to the next person.
- **Experience**: This is best done in a column format so it is easily read.
  - *Film* should be first with the project title in the first column. The role should be identified as *guest star, starring*, or *featured* rather than *soldier* or *woman,* which really doesn't tell us anything. The director or production company is the third column.
  - *TV* shows are second.
  - *Commercials* are next, and I usually just put *List upon request;* if you are auditioning for Toyota and you have Honda on the list, you don't want them to say "We can't hire her, she has a Honda

spot." Add details such as Cleo winner, or Super Bowl ads. If you worked with some prominent directors, name a few.

o ***Theatre*** should be in three columns, Play/Role/ Theatre- In this instance the actually role would be listed, such as Blanche in Street Car named desire at the Goodman Theatre

o ***Print*** or ***hosting*** go last; list the projects you were in

o ***Training:*** classes, schooling, workshops. Include your teachers and the name of the studio where you took the class.

o ***Special skills***: hobbies, anything you do *very well*. You have room to play around and stand out by putting something unusual about your-self (plays the spoons, or expert whistler) in addition to biking, hiking, and golf. If you are a golf pro with awards, of course you'd want to include that.

You want your résumé to be legible and not overpow-ering—and NEVER longer than one page. Trim the paper to 8 x 10 to exactly match the size of your headshot, then staple your headshot to the page. It's a disaster if the résumé becomes detached from the headshot and the casting director no longer knows who you are or how to reach you!

Actor/Actress Name

Acting agency and/or manager logo, name and contact information.

SAG-AEA-AFTRA

FILM

SAW XII	Mathilda	Lions Gate Films
AMERICAN PIE 9	Debbie	Universal Pictures
THE NANNY	Mrs. Wells	Indie Pictures
DAY JOB	Lead	Indie Feature - Dir. Amy Stuart
ENEMY AT THE DOOR	Lead	Indie Feature - Dir. Alan Ross
48 HOURS	Lead	Indie Feature - Dir. Bernard Gibbs
BREAKDOWN	Lead	Indie Feature - Dir. Mark Dupre
THE BRIDEGROOM	Supporting	Indie Feature - Dir. Cindy Johnson
STANISLAUS	Supporting	Indie Feature - Dir. Steve Stanford
THE 9:30 TRAIN	Supporting	Indie Feature - Dir. Yann Finn
CORNUCOPIA	Supporting	Indie Feature - Dir. Lulu Figgs
DESPERATE HUSBANDS	Supporting	Indie Feature - Dir. John Smith

TELEVISION

CSI	Recurring	CBS
BONES	Guest Star	FOX
COLD CASE	Guest Star	CBS
DESPERATE HOUSEWIVES	Guest Star	ABC
TWO AND A HALF MEN	Guest Star	CBS
UNTITLED PILOT	Series Regular	CBS
WOMEN OF THE WEST	Lead	MOW - Lifetime
STRONG MEDICINE	Guest Star	Lifetime
BABYLON 5	Guest Star	TNT
STARGATE ATLANTIS	Guest Star	SciFi Channel
LOST	Co-Star	ABC
24	Co-Star	NBC
SCRUBS	Co-Star	NBC
GREY'S ANATOMY	Co-Star	ABC
DEADWOOD	Co-Star	HBO
NCIS	Co-Star	CBS
MONK	Co-Star	NBC
GENERAL HOSPITAL	Recurring	ABC

THEATER

WIT	Susie Monahan	Ahmanson Theatre
ENCHANTED APRIL	Lotty Wilton	Pasadena Playhouse
BEIRUT	Blue	Kirk Douglas Theatre
MACBETH	Lady Macbeth	Laguna Playhouse
FALLEN ANGELS	Julia Sterroll	Geffen Playhouse
HEDDA GABBLER	Mrs. Elvsted	Mark Taper Forum
UNCLE VANYA	Helen	Actor's Gang Theatre
SUMMER AND SMOKE	Alma	Odyssey Theatre Ensemble
THE BABY DANCE	Wanda	Colony Theatre
THE MOUSETRAP	Miss Casewell	Odyssey Theatre Ensemble
DETECTIVE STORY	Mary McLeod	Blank Theatre Company
THE ART OF DINING	Nessa Vox	Blank Theatre Company

TRAINING

NAME OF SCHOOL (MFA in Acting)
Royal Academy of Dramatic Arts (London): 8-week intensive Shakespeare master class.
ACTING COACH: Name of coach.

SPECIAL SKILLS

Fluent in Spanish and French, dialect expert, dubbing and animation voice-over experience, swimming (competition level).

Copyright © Alexandra Swenson
All rights reserved.

Chapter 12

Your Team— Agents and Managers

Acting is behaving truthfully under imaginary circumstances.
—Sanford Meisner

Having an agent and/or manager is key to your success as an actor. In addition to getting you much-needed auditions, they are the gatekeepers to your reputation, and they are responsible for getting the word out about you and your talent. An agent or manager will keep you focused and on track.

Agents represent you, secure auditions for you, and negotiate bookings for you with terms for employment and payment based on how the spot will air (internet, cable, national network, and so forth).

You do very little in your career without an agent. You might be the exception, but most actors aren't known for their brilliant knowledge of business and contracts. Your agent is there to protect you—managing all negotiations and discussions with the casting directors, Production Company and union while protecting you and making sure you are being hired according to the agreed-upon terms.

Signing with a commercial agent is often easier than finding a theatrical agent. Commercial agencies handle all types of actors, all ages and skill sets. Many agencies are known for specializing in certain types of clients. For instance, Lemon Lime Agency is known for representing talent with a twist—their clients tend to be edgy and hip. Some agencies are known for handling pretty faces and yet others for ethnic types.

A manager is a great asset to an actor's career and a vital part of the team.

When a manager takes you on as a client, often she'll begin to develop you and shape your overall career. A manager often will secure a spot in an excellent but hard-to-crack agency for an appropriate client.

Typically, managers have fewer clients than agents, so they have more time to field questions, offer support for auditions, provide coaching if necessary or suggest great coaches prior to an audition..

I talk to my manager more often than my agent; her time constraints and business day are more flexible than those of an agent at a busy agency. Managers can talk to you about aspects of your career that are more personal, and you can establish a more intimate relationship.

Actors often have an agent for commercials, another agent for TV and film, and a manager who oversees every aspect of their acting careers.

Though it's possible to obtain auditions without an agent or manager, if you *really* want to work as a commercial actor, you need to sign with one or both. Only a handful of projects are released to the general population for public submission; most projects are sent exclusively to agents and some to managers.

To maximize your chances of getting called in for an audition, you need to be in the loop for all the projects.

Submissions these days are exclusively done online via LA Casting or Casting Frontier. The digital age has leveled the playing field for both agents and actors. An actress with little or no experience, represented by a boutique agency, could have her thumbnail headshot posted right next to the headshot of a veteran actress with a top-tier agent; depending on the project, they both may be called in.

In your pursuit of an agent, your main concern should be how excited the agent is about you and if he understands what's unique about you—if he really "gets you"—not how famous and powerful the agency is. The passion the agent has for you is critical, a key element in your success. You must be able to work with this person and be in a true partnership.

Finding an agent

Do your homework. This is where the business part of acting comes into play for you. Obtain a book on the various agencies in town and find out which ones to target. Ask your friends who reps them. Go on IMDB and search the client list yourself; ascertain what types of actors the agencies represent and where you might best fit in.

Before you start submitting or doing workshops, get your act together, literally.

Headshot. The headshot should look like you, on a good day but not on your best day. The chapter on head-shots goes into more detail; review it before you spend your money. Your headshots need to be professionally shot and professionally printed. Argentum Photo Lab or Pixels Digital Imaging both do a good job; their prints are always clear and the color is natural.

Résumé. Sample résumés are in the back of the book. Include both your phone and email and your Representation, if you have one

Market yourself. Know how you will be cast in commercials. Are you a nice Midwest mom, a character type, or perhaps a hipster? Watch commercials and find yourself in them. A one-day seminar or private coaching will be helpful in the discovery process. Accept and adopt your new castable self before meeting an agent so you can truly market yourself.

Dress for your type. If you're a character type—an uptight librarian, for example—don't meet your potential agent while wearing skinny jeans and a tank top. Dress to suggest you know who you are in commercials. If *you* don't know who you are, how will they know how to submit you?

Take a class. This suggestion is not only smart but necessary for the actor to present themselves in a good light. It shows you are eager, willing, and ready to be on the team.

It is a great conversation starter to say, "Hey, I just finished taking classes at Keep It Real Acting and feel *so* ready to apply all that I learned and start booking."

Agents respond well to actors who are ready to go out on auditions or who have a proven track record of booking.

Get a meeting with an agent

Take a commercial acting class or participate in an agent workshop

- Ask a friend for a referral to their agency
- Ask a casting director for a referral to an agency
- Mail or email submissions with a cover letter
- Network

Most commercial agents are now requiring referrals. You have heard the adage, *it's not what you know, but who you know.* Believe it or not, Los Angeles is a small town; who you know can make a difference. Having a referral from a teacher, coach or successful actor will certain help get you in the door . . . then the rest is up to you.

If you've booked jobs in the last few years, ask those casting directors if they would suggest an agency for you. They could help you immensely; even if they say "no," you've reconnected with someone in the business and they'll be more likely to remember you.

Mailing submissions is costly, and mail often sits unopened for weeks in busy agencies. Email can be effective; however, an unrecognized name can go unnoticed and is often deleted before reading. The best way to make contact is when agents or managers see your work and then invite you to come into the office and take a meeting.

There are many agent workshops in town; they can be an excellent use of funds and you hit several birds with one stone. The format is simple: Four or five agents attend a workshop where actors prepare and perform commercial auditions. I suggest you get coached prior to attending a workshop so you make a good lasting first impression with the agents. This is your opportunity to show them what you got. Don't be pennywise and pound foolish—invest the money in a coach to make sure your delivery is spot-on.

Many good commercial acting classes invite an agent or manager to attend the final class. The agents come looking for potential clients, and of course they see you in a more positive light because you're being proactive in your career. Even if they do not need your type at this particular time, it is a connection being made. Get their name and make sure you stay in touch.

Keep your eyes and ears open for news about agents—where they are, if they move to a different agency, and when they open their own. The timing may not be right at this time, but the connection is made.

Stay in touch with every connection you make.

The agent interview

It's time to prepare. Most actors think the work is done once they have secured an appointment with an agency. Now they just have to shower, put on something attractive and show up. *Wrong!* There is serious work to be done to insure you are putting your best foot forward. Your interview should end with the agent determined he *must* have you on the agency's roster.

Dress for the interview. Read the entire chapter devoted to *Your Castable Self*—it is critically important information. Dress for the interview; show the agent you know who you are in commercials. You need to help an agent figure out how to market you.

I have seen actresses go to the agent interview in tight, sexy clothing and get signed, only to find later they are being sent up only for those kinds of roles. They don't book them, because they're really not that type; then the agent drops them. The actor is left thinking, "My agent didn't see me as the comedic actress I am." Well, of course not; she gave her agent the wrong first impression.

You must typecast yourself. Most actors are terrified to

typecast themselves; they fear they will only be seen in this one light. However, you need to establish credibility and awareness of your talents. Remember, folks on the other side of the camera don't have huge imaginations. They see what they see and it sticks. Of course, over the course of your relationship with your agent, you can show him your other sides, and as you grow and change you can expand your types. When you begin, just stick to being typecast.

A talented actor took my commercial class; although his acting chops were good, his approach to the copy felt very false to me. When I asked him how he saw himself in commercials, he said he was a leading man, hero type, a spokesperson. He was just 5'8" tall with curly hair, very nebbish looking and quirky, definitely a character type. I gently said, "I think you would be better off playing character roles instead and grow into a type; then you'll have clout to be a spokesperson/hero type."

He looked sad and slightly defeated and went home. I thought about him all week, afraid I'd dashed his dreams although I had the best intentions in mind and meant to give him a leg up in this business. I was shocked and pleased when he came back the next week with a whole new outlook on himself, making a 180-degree U-turn, embracing his character image.

I am happy to report he went on to book a dozen commercials that year, he continues to work all the time, and his agent is thrilled with the change.

Drive the interview. Bluntly put, your job in the interview is to show your personality to the agent. If your prospective agent is looking down at your résumé and you are sitting there quietly, waiting for them to say something or to ask you a question, your interview is doomed. I coach actors to start talking as they walk down the hall to the interview room.

Find ways to talk about things that you are passionate about and can share some juicy details and specifics in regards to those subjects. *And DON'T talk about acting—* not right off the bat. What things make up who *you* are? Do you like to play tennis? Are you an avid hiker? Are you a shopper?

One actor *loved* to grocery shop even more than shopping for clothes. Before her agent meeting, I coached her to find out what stores were near the agent's office. On her way down the hall to her meeting, she said, "I love that your office is just a couple of blocks away from Whole Foods. I would never get any work done if I worked here. I would always run out for something. It is my favorite store. I spend hours in there touching all the vegetables and sampling all the healthy salads." The agent loved her candor and honest, real personality and signed her on the spot.

This is the best way to let the agent see you. You want them to fall in love with you, not your résumé. Let your personality out and let it lead the interview.

Ask a question. Hopefully, by now the agent is saying, "I have to have this person on my roster." This is the time for you to ask a question that shows you are smart and a savvy business person. You can let them know that you are meeting with a few more agents in the next few weeks but love the feeling here. It feels like a good fit. Simply say you would like to know:

- How does the office split up the submissions?
- Does more than one agent submit me?
- Do you generally use the main shot to submit?
- If you were to represent me, what age range would you submit me for?
- How do you communicate with your clients, other than audition notices?

Of course, you can ask any variation of these questions or something else entirely. Just make sure it's pertinent. Asking a question shows them you are not desperate and that you are a thoughtful, smart, actor who would be a pleasure to work with.

I've coached actors on this interview style for quite a while. Among those who successfully embrace it, it has a 98% success rate. After you sign with your new agent, you'll get more bookings because he already knows how to submit you.

Q&A with Commercial Agent of the Year, Hugh Leon

Hugh Leon of Coast to Coast Talent Group is an award-winning commercial agent, one of the best known and most respected agents in the country.

Judy: What do you look for in an actor who comes in for representation?

Hugh: There are four things that I typically look for when considering taking on a client:

Do you have a commercial look? I know this is subjective, but the first thing I need to evaluate is ***whether or not you are something I can sell.***

Do you fill a need for us or do we already have your category filled?

Can you handle copy and how do you handle direction? For instance, the buttons that actors come up with at the end of a read really make a difference; they can help separate you from the pack when the other actors are just saying the same lines.

Personality! Do I feel that you are going to be high maintenance? Are you somebody that I know I can send out there and be confident in your ability to do well, be professional, charming and personable? Finally, will your personality fit with how we work?

Judy: What do you tell actors after you sign them?

Hugh: We conduct a thorough orientation after signing. ***Both sides should know what we expect from them and what they expect from us.*** We make sure that they have the right photos and are enrolled in a good commercial class like yours, even if they already have training. I only recommend a few classes, and Keep it Real Acting is one of them. After you feel that you are at the top of your game, then do casting workshops/showcases. Also, improv training with one of the big stages like UCB, iO West or Second City.

Judy: What's the best way for actors to bolster their relationship with an agent?

Hugh: The best way to foster a good agent relationship is to comply with what we ask. Make sure you have the right materials, always make sure your cell phone is turned on and with you at all times; stay available for auditions as much as possible, and if you're not going to be available, give us adequate notice; have a flexible job that allows you to make your auditions; and stay on top on your game.

Always remember: We are 10% and you are 90% . . . what are you doing for your 90%?

We don't always have time for actors to drop by. Instead, shoot us emails to let us know what you're working on or the big events in your life. It's important to keep in touch without being over-burdening or obnoxious.

Judy: What tips would you give to an actor who is in a slump (not booking)?

Hugh: They have to understand that when they are going through a slump and it starts to mess with their confidence, maybe they are down about personal stuff or just reaching too hard for a booking. This is very difficult to conceal and is reflected in their performance. Their confidence is not the same.

Find a way to reach within, to concentrate on the positives, even if there aren't many. You may even have to remind yourself, "I'm talented," "I have my house," "I have my friends." Find something on the inside that really shines through to make the confidence and inner light shine again. The people that are booking are the people out there that are just having fun and not getting in their own heads. They found peace and happiness and they just shine!

Get into a class and you'll find breakthroughs! You'll be able to watch yourself on tape. The class itself has other actors in it going through similar career swings. It'll give you the opportunity to get out of your head and have someone point things out and notice the little things that are there and what may be missing.

Judy: What is the most rewarding and fulfilling part of being an agent?

Hugh: When a client books a job . . . helping them fulfill their dreams. When an actor gets really excited, that makes me happy! Show some enthusiasm—it makes me want to have you book again. One of the most fulfilling experiences is when someone is in a slump, we have a little pep talk, and then they go out to book!

Judy: What advice would you give to actors who are without representation?

Hugh: There are a lot of actors who aren't represented, so make sure you stand out. Many actors put the cart before the horse and aren't ready for an agent yet. Actors should research what makes a quality commercial head shot and what that entails... Actors should also have commercial training—not just theatrical training.

Have your ducks in a row, know your business and get your feet wet before you even approach representation. Do your research. Get to know who you are approaching and how you are coming across. You can't just show up on a baseball field and say "Ok, I want to be in the major leagues!" Why should an agent represent you? Give them a reason to do so.

About Hugh Leon

Hugh is a partner and head of the adult commercial and celebrity departments at Coast to Coast Talent Group, one of the leading talent agencies in Los Angeles since 1987. Coast to Coast represents youth and adult actors for commercials, print, voice over and film/TV.

Hugh has been an active participant in the entertainment industry for over four decades. He began his show business career as a child actor in Philadelphia before moving to New York City, and later to Los Angeles. After graduating from UCLA, he worked at a couple of agencies before joining Coast to Coast in 1996.

Hugh's lifelong experience in show business has contributed to his unparalleled success in representing commercial and celebrity talent. He has been nominated by the TMA (Talent Managers Association) TEN consecutive years, and won three Commercial Agent of the Year Seymour Heller awards (2007, 2012, & 2013). Hugh has also been featured in numerous television program interviews, and is quoted in countless national industry publications.

Chapter 13

The Director and the Producer

Acting is always at the core of my life, but I'm also excited about producing. I'm excited about directing, and I have a life in the filmmaking world, and so I want to explore all aspects of it, not just the acting, but acting is the root.

—Nicolas Cage

Q&A with commercial director Kevin Emmons

The commercial director is hired by the production company and/or the client, based on the style in which he directs and his special niche talents.

Directors often have big input, sometimes even the final decision, on who will be cast in a spot. Directors often like to work with actors they know and whom they have worked with before.

When he directs you in the callback, the director has an opportunity to see what you're like to work with and if his concept for the commercial is working. He'll give you notes and suggestions on how to play certain aspects of the scene.

Judy: You know how to talk to actors. Your background as a cameraman gives you so much more edge as a director. Take us through how YOU get a job.

Kevin: Typically with commercials, the common route is an ad agency or a client like Coca Cola with an ad agency. The agency presents an idea—let's say, young hipsters dancing on a rooftop in L.A., drinking Coca Cola. They seek out a production company with a director. The process is to look at reels and decide who has the vibe of the spot. Maybe it is a lifestyle spot, or music-driven, or vintage. They may look at 50 reels of directors over as long as six weeks, slowly gathering their ideas. Finally they narrow it down to four or five directors and then they do a conference call with final cut. The creative team (copywriter, art director, the creative director, agency producer of some sort) feel out the directors on the phone and ask them what their take on the spot is and how excited it makes them.

Then they ask three directors to bid the job. There are two components—the creative part and the money part.

So the director's production team gets together and makes a bid. If the creative team wants a crane shot or rooftop shot, for example, they factor that in. Somehow the creative team, the production company, and the director have a rough idea and an agreement, and they do a bid.

Many times I will have to write a treatment: What is the look, the feel, the kind of music I hear? All of this gets presented in a document that I might work on one for up to four or five days, and I don't get paid for it.

Much like an actor who goes to an audition, you might go to 100 auditions and land one so-so spot, but that is part of your job and part of the industry. I don't care who you are, you have to audition. The more you audition, the better you get at it. My number one pet peeve is that young actors look at auditions as a pain or a frustration. "I did ten auditions and I never make the final cut."

I can tell you, there are a lot of times I see the same hundred people, and the same ten make the final cut. There is something they are doing right.

Let's say you're lucky enough to get chosen to be the director, and then you start working with that creative team. You get a schedule. You're going to audition the first week in April, you're shooting the first week in May, and you're prepping and looking at locations.

It is a constant overlap of projects. For instance, I was filming yesterday on a soundstage. As soon as we wrapped, I went back to the hotel for a conference call for a job that might or might not happen a month from now. I am finishing up a few treatments for other jobs that might or might not happen, and I have a meeting about a potential spot that may or may not happen. My life is I'm either shooting, prepping or crossing my fingers applying for a job—much being like an actor.

Judy: What can actors do to improve their auditions?
Kevin: Look, feel, and dress the part, from the moment you walk into the room with your head space in the part. The agency people are watching. If it is comedic, then by all means be funny.

Who are the people that stand out? The ones that make eye contact and make a connection as a human to human. Ultimately, you are not only auditioning, but you are showing who you are as a person.

My number two pet peeve is when actors rush through the slate and profile, and they don't smile.

We want to see you, whether or not you're out of shape. Sometimes that is why you get picked. Embrace who you are . . . *all* your quirks. It is not about being perfect. We often look for the quirky.

Present yourself. Take your time in the slate, in the understanding of the role. And if it is a scripted part, take the time to know it. *Not* in a memorized robotic fashion, because we don't want to see a reading, either. But understand the script and know the content. When someone blows us away in a casting, it is because they took the time to become familiar with the material. **That is your**

homework. Everybody has some kind of homework in life. The actor is usually a very undisciplined person. I see actors who book all the time, and it is because they are working hard.

Don't worry about the run of the spot. You are making connections. *Do the work* and the rest of it will fall into place.

I think the most frustrating parts of the process of selecting and finding talent are:

- How often actors are unprepared. Someone who does a lot of commercial work gets better and better at it.
- How they don't understand the role they are seeking. What does it say? The agency and the director come up with specs for the casting office, so they will write the description of the character. Pay attention.
- How they don't dress for the part. Come to the casting appropriately dressed; you would be surprised how often people come dressed inappropriately. Do you know what a hipster looks like? He's not a conservative 60-year-old in pinstripes.
- Callbacks! Let's say 100 people auditioned, I have six favorites and the agency has eight favorites. Sometimes they overlap and you have commonality. Now, if they have eight chosen for callback, and I have eight, and they are completely different, I get concerned that their vision of the commercial

is different than mine. Still, if 16 people come to the callback and you end up with a great actor, it's excellent!

Judy: What about copy? How important is it?
Kevin: If it's scripted, take the time to learn it. I don't want you to memorize it. Just work on it. I have seen people sitting in the lobby who are not working in the lobby; they are just talking, and once they get to the room, they are just reading the lines.

Do your homework and your chances will improve. People who are working are working hard. Don't worry about how it is airing. The connection you make is what is important.

Let's say you're just going to commercial work to make money. A lot of people downgrade what commercials can do for you. I think what you need to say to yourself is, "I am a working actor and will be invested in the working and think of it as a business." How are you bettering your career?

Judy: What happens when you pick an actor?
Kevin: I have three or four criteria.

- They have to look and feel the part. That can be heavily weighted sometimes; it may be the sole reason.
- Depending on what I know is expected of them, I ask myself, "Will this person be fun to work with?

Will they be enjoyable on the set?" I have to imagine the shoot. For instance, an actor might have to be on a boat and a bike. What will they be like? Nothing is worse than an actor who is complaining.

- We have all heard stories about models; it is not so glamorous when you're in a bathing suit on a rooftop in 40-degree weather.
- Do they go above and beyond in terms of their work?
- Will this person make me look good?

When it comes to callbacks, hopefully at the end of the day, we can cull it down and three gems pop out. Sometimes we just know in the callback who's the one. The actor does their audition and leaves the room; we just look at each other and say, "That's the person!" Even after we're forced to look at the other 15, rarely am I swayed.

We choose the final one to three actors. We come to an agreement on the number one choice and present this to the client: This is our recommended actor and here are our back-ups.

As a director, you may have to fight for someone. Sometimes I will ask the casting director about the actor and he can help sway the choice because he does this every day and has done it for years and years. Often I will ask for others' opinions and I try to hone in on what I want.

Sometimes people will get hung up on funny things. Once I wanted to cast an actor but the creative team got hung up on his glasses. I asked him if he could read without the glasses, and he said, "I can't see—but I also wear contacts." I sent him home to get his contacts, and he got the part.

Judy: When you say you know they're the ones when they walk in the room—do these actors make the scene their own?

Kevin: *Yes, yes, yes!* A lot of times. Let's say the part is for an uptight librarian, and maybe in the commercial all she is going to do is be an uptight librarian. Yet, at the end of the audition, she pulls her hair down and does an extra 20%. How great is that? Yes, often it is the littlest teeny thing that gets them ahead of the pack.

I typically have actors do two to three takes, but if it is an MOS spot, I will do an interview. I'll say, "Where did you grow up?" Don't just answer, "Omaha, Nebraska," do something else! Add a personal story. Say, "Actually, I am a farm girl, and my vision of LA was funny . . .'cause all I had seen was corn fields . . .'cause I am from Omaha."

Say something that tells me more of your personality. We get you. Did you light up?

When you're selling yourself, you need to have a handle on what you can add to make you shine. I often do these interviews, and I ask questions to get an idea of your personality. Once I had a girl who never once answered a question I asked. It was so funny—I remembered I must have asked five questions and she never directly answered one of them.

Taboos. Unless you're told, wear the same thing for a callback as you wore for the original audition. Sometimes a slight change is fine, but don't change yourself so much that I don't recognize why I called you back.

Once I had a guy with a beard; when he came back and he'd shaved and unfortunately we couldn't use him.

Be careful about changing before the callback! Nothing radical!

Let's say I saw a particular actress that I thought had a particular quirky vibe. On her callback, she is completely stressed and apprehensive. Suddenly we saw she wasn't so great. *Every time* you walk into the room, you have to know how to leave your outside stuff outside, and come in with the same vibe.

The script. The casting director has provided the script, and basically this is what you're going to say to camera. *All* we ever care about, though—*and I cannot say it enough!*— is the general intent.

If you stand there and keep correcting yourself and say, "Oh, I am sorry. I am sorry!" and keep doing takes, at some point you lose us.

Now on the shoot day, that is different. You have to get it right.

A lot of time, the copy is completely secondary. Some-time I have the actors tell me the copy in their own words.

The least important thing to me is the copy—*unless it is technical copy!* Then you have to do your homework and we need to know you're going to get it out. You also do have the name of the product correctly.

The worst thing you can do is be difficult—be late, be snarky, be needy. Come to work and work hard, and the director will remember that.

Years later I will see actors with whom I have worked, and I will say in casting that I have worked with them before and they give 100 percent. This matters.

I don't care if it is a tiny little web video, because people remember. This is the same is for an audition.

Once I picked two girls who go into a shoe store for an ad; the person I wanted to cast for the lead wasn't chosen, and she worked as an extra. Still she listened, and was more attentive than the leads, and I noticed her hard work. A few months later, I saw her for another spot and made sure she got the part. Since then, I have worked with her a few more times.

It's all about working.

About Kevin Emmons

Raised a military brat, Kevin traveled and lived extensively throughout the U.S. From a young age, he carried a camera with him everywhere to document his travels. Photography became a lifelong passion.

After graduating from college with a degree in Film/Theater, Kevin spent several years traveling the world filming documentaries in China, Russia, Tibet and Cuba (to name just a few locales), crafting works that aired on PBS and major networks.

Continuing his passion for cinematography, he moved on to the world of advertising, shooting everything from food to fashion, sports, athletes, celebrities, effects and lifestyle spots.

One of the few commercial directors of photography inducted into the prestigious Society of Operating Cameramen (SOC), Kevin has been cinematographer on well over 1,500 national television commercials for such diverse clients as Reebok, Ford, Kraft, Coke, McDonald's, and Budweiser, and some spots were aired as coveted Super Bowl ads. His images have won awards at local and national levels including snagging Addy, Telly and Clio awards.

Kevin has written articles for several industry publications, is a Director of Photography in local 600, and most recently became a member of the Directors Guild of America.

Currently, Kevin has found a niche directing commercials that are best described as "stylized documentary," concentrating on fashion and lifestyle commercials.

Q&A with commercial producer Anton Maillie

The producer is hired by the production company to oversee all aspects of creating the commercial, including keeping it on budget. The producer assembles the team of many players, including the crew, craft service, location scouts, lighting designers, costumers etc.

Although producers have some say in the talent selected, they usually defer to the client and the director. They don't hesitate to give input on actors they've worked with before, whether the experience was good or bad.

Judy: What is your main job as a producer?
Anton: I am kind of a two-fold producer. There are producers who are more financial- and schedule-minded, and there are ones who are more creative-minded.

Then there are producers who produce the way I do. I feel like I do it all in equal parts. I love the creative, so I am there to support the director and the agency, to deliver the best possible spot even if it costs us a little more money to do it right.

It is a balance of three things:

- Protecting the production company—making sure they make their profit margin so they can stay in business and you're asked to come back.
- Looking out for the director and sometimes actually keeping him from destroying his own career and his egomaniacal relationships.

- Taking care of the agency. You always want the agency to come back . . . you want the repeat business. It's definitely part of the equation to keep any business healthy.

Sometimes I will arm wrestle with this one director because he'll get into my production soup and I'll get into his creative soup. We will arm wrestle, but it is a loving working relationship.

With some directors, I don't say a peep about creative. I just stick to putting the job together. So what that entails is trying to match up who and what is right for the job. If it is a car job, a beauty commercial, a visual effects spot, it means getting the right DPs, casting director, location scout who may be more savvy in finding a rock quarry as opposed to a front lawn of someone's house.

Then I build the macro schedule, saying, "Okay, we have nine locations to shoot in three days; what is the best way to skin this? Let's find three anchor locations we know we need, and then build the other locations around that." The same thing goes for trying to piece in the expensive equipment for the right days.

You balance in all those things. Every once in a while you get conflicts, a talent who has a schedule, and you try to accommodate all those things. Then I hand it off to the AD once I break down the days.

I have relationships. Relationship are important to me. I have lists of scouts, teamsters, gang bosses, and casting directors who are my priority, and production managers who make me look good.

There's no yelling on my sets, no egos. It is a family.

I have had to fire people just a few times in 25 years. In commercials, you shoot in one to five days—you just don't hire them back.

Judy: What do you love about the producer's job?
Anton: I like being in charge! Seriously, as a producer I'm either the most important person on set or I'm just a glorified secretary; it depends on the day and the personalities involved. I am not a 9-to-5 person. I am not an office person. I couldn't do the same job every day.

Though there is a lot of repetition and familiarity in what we do—prepping, shooting and wrapping jobs—each job has its own excitement, even if it's a small budget job. I love the travel, and I have been so fortunate—I have shot over 30 overseas jobs.

I love the challenge, I really do, trying to figure out how to make it work, especially now with the budgets shrinking. They want the same material delivered for less money. There are so many reasons for this. A lot had to do with the economy turning sour 7-8 years ago. Also, a lot of agencies are spreading their money thinner to cover other media platforms.

One year they may have a million dollars for four spots in a four-day shot, and the next year they are trying to get it done for $900,000—and they get it done because there is enough competition out there. Someone is going do it, whether you take half a loaf or you don't take any at all. Before you know it, over the course of five years, what you used to do for $1 million, now you have to do for $400,000.

Judy: How does a producer get jobs, Anton?

Anton: For the most part, it is through the directors. I may get in with a director through an executive producer, like the owner of the company. I'll give you an example: I used to know this agency producer who went over to the production side, and she represents director James Mangold, who directed *Walk the Line* and *Girl Interrupted*. They were looking for a producer for him last year, so I met with the owner of the company who said, "You would be a great match for Mangold." He and I ended up working together on two jobs and I have another job with him coming up shortly.

It also could be through another producer who turns down a job with their director because he is not available. We have a little network of producers who refer each other to other directors because we know they won't try to steal them from us—they will be respectful of the relationship. The director may wind up liking them better, but I can't control that.

Judy: What skills do you have that make you a producer?

Anton: *Knowing how to juggle.* I learned that from my

mom. Definitely, knowing how to juggle 20 balls in the air at once and knowing which one has to be addressed first—kind of letting water finding its own level at times.

Not forcing a solution. Take care of these bits of business and the solution will present itself.

Being inherently good with numbers. In my head, there is a little calculator running that knows what I am spending, so I am never really surprised. I know I can sign off on this location for $2000 more than I want to pay because I know I have it somewhere else.

Definitely keeping a financial eye on things.

Also, I know how to make pieces fit well together.

Judy: Take us behind the scenes at an audition.

Anton: From where I sit, next to the director and with three or four agency people by my side, we look for actors who are themselves. We don't want to see someone putting on a show, over-greeting people. On the other end of the spectrum, we don't want someone who looks disinterested. We want them to want to *be* there, *do* their job, *listen* to the director, and *give it their best shot* at their performance.

I see actors lose roles for so many of the wrong reasons. You may have been the best one in there, definitely the best person for the role, but then one person in the agency says you really don't look like that kid's mom, and all of a sudden the best person just lost the role. It is a shame when you see someone nail it yet not get it for the wrong reasons.

Judy: Show us a peek behind the curtain of the casting process and selection.

Anton: I have some directors who will only call back one or two people, five to six max—they know who they are looking for. Other directors will call back 20-30 per role, the agency picks 20-30 per role, and as the producer it is my job is to do a flow chart to see the crossovers and who was a favorite of everyone.

Everyone has their sheets with their rating system, and we lay them out on a big table and say "I really love . . ."

The person you audition with can often help you if you are lucky enough to get paired up with someone who enhances your audition. It is a plus! Sometimes it can hurt you if you're paired with someone who is not that good or right for the role, but most directors can see through it and say "she was great; he sucked."

We take all the headshots of the people we like and lay them out. We will kind of assemble a family. For the most part, we get it right. There is not just one good choice for each role. Sometimes there could be three or four great choices for a role. When someone doesn't get the part, it's not because they are any worse or better, it's just that someone had to be picked.

Occasionally, someone comes in with attitude, and

she may get pushed to the bottom of the pile. Occasionally, someone comes in and it seems like they don't want to be there. A lot of it comes down to who looks right and has the acting skill and is in the right age range. They'll nail it.

We always pick two, sometimes three, depending on the client.

Judy: Who has the final pick?

Anton: The client always has the final pick. The director and the agency do their first and second choice, and often it goes to the next level—which is the creative director who is back in NY at the agency or the head of the agency, and he may say "Yeah, I like all your picks, but I don't like this person." For no rhyme or reason, they just need to flex their muscle. Every once in a while, the director really wants someone; he will get on the phone to the agency and say, "I really pick this woman because of A, B, and C," and they will say, "Okay, go with her." A lot of times that phone call never happens, so the person we really like in the room gets nixed by a creative director.

And then it goes to the client and they look through and have the final say.

Judy: How does an actor get known?

Anton: You can always tell when you get a good cast.

Things just gel so nicely. There are jobs when I can't remember a single actor on the job, and then there are jobs when I remember every single actor because I really bonded with them as a producer.

Like right now if we had to cast a commercial, I would put some of my favorite people up for it. I would tell my casting director, "Let's bring in these nine actors, because not only were they good, but a pleasure to work with. They felt like a part of the team."

Most actors are humble, believe or not, even though they are self-obsessed. They want to be a part of the crew, be a part of the experience, because they have a hard job. Acting is the hardest job on the set.

On the flip side of that, there are some actors who I never want to see on my set again. I will pull the director aside and say, "I worked with this guy, and he is just a nightmare, a pain in the ass the entire time."

"Pain in the ass" means just *difficult*. Not necessarily talking back to the director, just not listening and getting the director's direction. Some are belligerent; they are not pleasant people and kind of kill the mood on the set.

You want someone to deliver a great performance first, and second, you want to enjoy the experience of working with them. It's fantastic when you put a cast together and they meld together beautifully.

We had four actor/stuntmen doing some very simple slips and slides. Three of the stuntmen were just loving it, and the fourth guy tried to complicate things. He was a pain in the ass. That is the most annoying thing an actor can do.

Judy: Do you have some final words of advice?
Anton: Even if you feel you're not right for the role, take the audition. If nothing else, you get experience auditioning. This is super important. You can see the contrast between someone coming in for the first time who is a little nervous, and someone coming in for the same role who has been there 20 times before. The experienced ones just have a little bit more of a relaxed attitude. That favors them a little.

It is a hard job. You may have been the best person in that room, but for whatever reason, two others were equally as terrific.

People have short memories. Very few will remember a seeing a bad audition.

You can get the role two ways:
1. You have the right look, though you may not have the best range or set of skills of all the actors who auditioned.
2. You have the best set of skills, though your look may be off a little bit for what they visualized.

If you have both the skills and the look, it is a slam dunk. Still, you can get squashed for all the wrong reasons.

Judy: Does the casting director have much input?
Anton: Casting directors are super important, because they

can take a spec and if they do the job right, they can really enhance it. They can bring in people who may not normally be thought of for that role. I value a good casting director very much; they make my life much easier.

The casting director may turn to me and say, "I know we are looking for a 13-year-old boy with braces, but there really are not a lot out there; are you open to girls?"

I will say, "Great idea! Yes, do it. Bring in 50-50 girls and boys." Often the director and agency will forget the original specs they gave me and go with the girl.

About Anton Maillie

Anton went to college for accounting for two weeks . . . until he discovered a film major existed. He then spent four years at the University of Miami doing TV, radio and broadcasting, learning to make films, write and direct.

He found his strength was editing, and when he graduated, he went to New York, working as an assistant editor for a year. He woke up one day and said to himself, "I didn't get into this to do editing. I want to move to California and get into production." So he packed up the next day and moved to California.

He was fortunate and found a job on a feature as a PA, which led to two more features. One of the directors he worked with produced commercials, and as soon as he worked with him on his first commercial, he knew "that was it," and quickly moved up to coordinating and production managing.

He started working freelance with Backyard Productions in 1996, and worked with a wide variety of directors for about ten years. When some of the directors moved on, so did he. Two years ago, he put a website together, and it exploded to where he's turning down three or four jobs a month now. The website completely changed the dynamics of finding jobs.

Glossary

Key terms to know in commercial acting

audition. An interview for a particular role as a commercial actor, consisting of a practical demonstration of the candidate's suitability and skill.

beat. "Take a beat" means *take a brief pause*. A beat is a change in the scene, beginning a new moment; it can be a change in either action or thought.

brand. A name, term, design, symbol or feature that distinguishes one product from another—or one actor from another.

buttons. Three words or less that you add to the end of a scene to keep the action going naturally (also see *tags*).

callbacks. The second round of auditions in which the director, client and agency people are in attendance.

castable self. The essence that sets you apart from every actor in your category.

casting director. Hired by the production company or commercial director to find the talent for a commercial. The casting director posts a breakdown, or description of the castable types needed for the commercial, and narrows down the 3000 actors submitted by their agents and managers to about 100 or less, primarily by reviewing headshots.

cheat out. Facing the camera instead of your scene partner. This allows you to be taped full-face rather than in profile.

copy. Also known as the script. Written by the client's agency, and the starting point for all commercials with spoken words.

costume. The outfits you keep on hand for your various castable roles. A costume should evoke a particular character.

essence. The inward nature, true personality, or constitution of a person. It's how you come off on camera.

equity waiver. A show played in a theater with fewer than 100 seats is allowed to hire non-union actors and/or pay union actors less than equity level wages.

filmic. As applied to commercials, it means shot in the style of a feature film.

fourth wall. The imaginary wall that separates actors from their audience. It was first used when stages or sets were traditional three-walled boxes. For the commercial actor, it refers to the imaginary wall where the camera is positioned.

headshot. An 8x10 picture that shows what you look like and what you are. This is how you are chosen for an audition. The shot should show you just from the shoulders up. When your picture is online—which is when the casting director sees it—your headshot is the size of a thumbprint. The larger printed versions are also attached to your resumes.

high resolution (hi rez). High-quality cameras should be used for your headshots (along with a high-quality photographer!), and the images saved in detailed, or high-resolution, images. You want your personality to shine through, which it can't do in a blur of oversize pixels.

improv. Short for improvisation, or making it up as you go along. A type of audition, also an acquired and necessary skill for actors,

indicate. Bluntly, it means emoting falsely, "without being connected to a truthful impulse. In other words, over-acting.

low resolution (low rez). Point-and-shoot cameras and cellphones take low-rez pictures. When blown up or viewed online, they have little detail and don't stand out. Even good, high-quality images can be saved as low-rez images—make sure you don't do this with your headshots.

MOS. A nonverbal audition. MOS is traditionally said to come from a famous German-speaking director saying, "Mit out sound."

motivate out. Finding a reason (or motivation) to look at the camera or fourth wall while auditioning.

notes. Comments from the director.

personality question. A form of audition where you're asked to answer a random question, not act in a scene. Your goal is to show your personality when you answer the questions.

personalize. The single most important thing you can do is make everything you refer to *personal*. Use your life experience when you talk about your kids—or your laundry detergent.

scene. A form of audition where you interact with one or more other actors.

selly. Overtly trying to promote the product.

session director. The director who's hired by the casting director to get the best from each actor during the audition.

sides. The lines from the script you learn prior to an audition, and any other information about the spot that allows you to prepare.

slating. Stating your name into the camera prior to the audition scene. The formal act of introducing yourself to the director, the camera, the agency and the client who will be watching your audition tape.

spokesperson. A sole actor in a commercial spot, also a term for a type of audition. The spokesperson is typically the character who speaks on behalf of the product.

tags. A few words added to the spot after the last scripted line. They should be the next thing you would say if the scene had continued (also see *buttons*).

uniform. The clothes you keep on hand to audition for certain types of roles.

About the Author

A professional actress for 38 years, Judy has show-cased her skills and talents in hundreds of commercials and film and television roles as well as transformed count-less actors' careers with her two schools.

Judy co-founded **Talent To Go,** a training company that won *The Best Casting Director Workshop in LA* award in 2009 and 2010. She continued her teaching legacy and success when she opened **Keep It Real Acting** in 2012, an award-winning full-service acting studio that offers commercial and theatrical classes for all levels of students. She was voted *Backstage West's Favorite On-Camera Commercial Teacher in LA* in 2010, 2011, and 2012 and again in 2015. Several of her classes have also won *Backstage West's Favorite in LA* awards, and the school continues to produce amazing results for her students.

Judy's hundreds of well-known credits include a SAG-award-winning recurring role on the Emmy-winning show

Mad Men as Olive Healey (Peggy's secretary). Other favorite recurring credits include **Odd Couple** with Matthew Perry, **Hand of God** with Ron Pearlman, **Married with Children, For Your Love, Grosse Pointe**, and **Manhattan, AZ** with Chad Everett.

Judy has done numerous guest appearances on the hit shows **Modern Family, The Middle, Bones, Castle, Rizzoli & Isles, Scrubs, Desperate Housewives, ER, Seinfeld, The District, The West Wing, NYPD Blue, Friends,** and **The Drew Carey Show** among others.

Her more than 375 commercial credits include several career highlights. Her role as judge in the famous Clairol Herbal Essence ad with Dr. Ruth was famously (and hilariously) spoofed on Saturday Night Live. She appeared in two acclaimed Super Bowl ads in 2013, Oreo's Whisper Fight ad and Deon Sanders' NFL promo.

The proud mother of one son, Frankie Manes, Judy resides in Los Angeles.

15878588R00090

Printed in Great Britain
by Amazon